THE INSTANT ORACLE

Predicting the Future Without a Horoscope

Kanav Sachdev

White Light Publication

The characters and events portrayed in this book are fictitious. Any similarity to real persons, living or dead, is coincidental and not intended by the author.

ISBN-13: 978-81-996899-0-9 (Hardcover)
ISBN-13: 978-81-997518-9-7 (Paperback)
ISBN-13: 978-81-993857-2-6 (Ebook)

Cover design by: Jyoti Sachdeva

Dedication To The Questioner, Who stands at the crossroads of fate, Not knowing which path leads to gold and which to ruin. To The Breath, The silent spy that enters every room before you do, And whispers the secrets of the enemy in your ear. And to Shiva, The Lord of Time, Who hid the map of the universe Right under our nose. Om Namah Shivaya.

CONTENTS

INTRODUCTION

"You have a clock. Now you need a compass."

In *Book 1: The Living Clock*, we learned to master Time. We learned to synchronize our biology with the rhythm of the Sun and Moon. We learned to optimize our energy, heal our bodies, and stop fighting the tide. That was the foundation. That was **Self-Mastery**.

But you do not live in a vacuum. You live in a chaotic, unpredictable, multiplayer game.

- You meet strangers who might be friends or enemies.
- You face decisions that have no clear answer.
- You lose things. You get lost. You get attacked.

Book 1 taught you *when* to act. Book 2 teaches you *what* will happen when you do.

This book is **The Instant Oracle**. It is based on the forbidden section of the *Shiva Swarodaya* known as **Prashna Shastra** (The Science of Questions). For centuries, this knowledge was reserved for Kings and Generals. They didn't use it to meditate. They used it to win wars. They used it to uncover spies. They used it to find stolen treasure.

They didn't need a horoscope. They didn't need to wait for a priest to calculate the stars. They just checked their breath.

In this book, we strip away the superstition and reveal the mechanics of **Immediate Divination**. We will turn your nervous system into a high-fidelity radar.

- You will learn to look at a client and know instantly if they will pay you or cheat you.

- You will learn to walk into a room and find the exact spot that guarantees authority.
- You will learn to predict the outcome of a romance simply by hearing the person's name.

This is not magic. It is **Biological Physics**. The universe is broadcasting data 24/7. Your breath is the receiver. If you know how to tune the frequency, you will never be blind again.

Welcome to the Oracle.

DISCLAIMER

Please read this disclaimer carefully before using this book or applying any of the principles described herein.

Fictionalization and Privacy

The case studies, anecdotes, and personal stories presented within this book are included for educational and illustrative purposes only. While they are inspired by real-world concepts and experiences, they are fictionalized. In all instances, the names, identifying details, professions, locations, and other key details of individuals have been altered or entirely fabricated to protect privacy and ensure anonymity. Any resemblance to actual persons, living or dead, or actual events is purely coincidental.

Not Professional Advice

The content of The Instant oracale is intended to provide information, spiritual concepts, and personal development principles based on the author's interpretation of ancient texts and practices. It is not intended to be a substitute for professional medical advice, diagnosis, or treatment.

- Consult a Professional: Always seek the advice of your physician or other qualified health provider with any questions you may have regarding a medical condition or before undertaking any new breathing or physical practice, particularly those involving breath retention or physical implements (such as the Yoga Danda).

- Use at Your Own Risk: The practices described in this book should be approached with respect and caution. The author and publisher are not responsible for any adverse effects or consequences resulting from the use of any suggestions, practices, or preparations mentioned in this book. Your engagement with the material is entirely at your own risk.

HOW TO USE THIS BOOK

Warning: This is a Dangerous Tool. Book 1 was safe. It was about health and routine. Book 2 is sharp. It deals with power, influence, and the decoding of other people's destinies.

The Rules of Engagement:

1. **Do Not Obsess:** When you first learn these techniques, you will want to check your nose every 5 minutes. Do not become a "Breath Neurotic." Use the Oracle only for *significant* questions. If you ask the Oracle what to eat for lunch, you dilute your intuition.
2. **Trust the First Signal:** The breath often shifts the moment you become anxious about the answer. The valid reading is the *immediate* one—the split second the question arises.
3. **The "Live Fire" Exercises:** At the end of each sub-chapter, you will find "Somatic Labs." You must do them. You cannot learn to taste the Elements by reading about them. You have to actually lick the air.

The Structure:

- **Chapter 1 (The Binary):** We learn the "Yes/No" code.
- **Chapter 2 (The Hologram):** We add color and shape (Elements).
- **Chapter 3 (The Compass):** We add direction and location.
- **Chapter 4 (The Sound):** We decode names and words.
- **Chapter 5 (The Void):** We learn to use the empty space as a

weapon.

By the end of this book, you will not need to ask anyone for advice. You will carry the answer in your pocket.

Let's begin.

CHAPTER 1: THE BINARY ORACLE (THE YOGA OF YES OR NO)

1.1: The Physiology of the Flow – The Cosmic Needle

> *"O Devi, the breath is the messenger of the future. The Right is the Sun, the Left is the Moon. When the question arises, look to the flow. If the flow is full (Purna), the door is open. If the flow is empty (Shunya), the door is closed. This is the only horoscope a Yogi needs." — Shiva Swarodaya*

Forget the crystal ball. Forget the Tarot cards. Forget the complex astrological charts that require your exact birth time down to the second. These are tools of mediation. They place an object between you and the Truth.

The **Swara Yogi** needs no mediation. The Swara Yogi carries the Oracle inside his own skull. It is ticking 24 hours a day, updating its prediction every second based on the shifting gravity of the cosmos. It is the **Breath**.

In Book 1, we learned to use the breath to manage our energy. In Book 2, we learn to use the breath to **interrogate reality**. We are entering the domain of **Prashna Shastra** (The Science of Questioning). When a question arises in your mind—*"Will this deal close?" "Does she love me?" "Is this investment safe?"*—the universe has already encoded the answer in your nervous system. The answer is binary. **Yes** or **No**. **Success** or **Failure**. **Full** or **Empty**.

This entire system of divination rests on one fundamental physiological fact: **One nostril is always dominant.** One side is the "Live Wire" (Purna). The other side is the "Dead Wire" (Shunya).

If you can accurately identify which wire is live at the exact moment a question is asked, you can predict the future with terrifying accuracy. But if you misread the flow—if you mistake the Dead Wire for the Live Wire—you will be wrong every time. You will bet on a losing horse. You will trust a liar. You will fight a war you cannot win.

Sub-Chapter 1.1 is the boot camp for the Oracle. We are going to debunk the myths of "equal breathing." We are going to refine your sensitivity until you can feel the difference between a 51% flow and a 49% flow. And we are going to establish the **Golden Rule of Divination**: *Follow the Flow.*

Part I: The Anatomy Of The Binary – Why The Universe Splits

To understand why the breath predicts the future, you have to understand the nature of Reality. We live in a **Dualistic Universe** (Dvaita).

- Day / Night
- Hot / Cold
- Male / Female
- Success / Failure
- Yes / No

This duality is not just "out there." It is hardwired into your body. The **Ida (Left/Moon)** and **Pingala (Right/Sun)** are the biological antennas for this duality. At any given moment, your body is prioritizing one polarity over the other.

- If the **Right Nostril** is open, your body is saying: *"I am ready to OUTPUT. I am ready to Act, Consume, Destroy, and Project."*
- If the **Left Nostril** is open, your body is saying: *"I am ready to INPUT. I am ready to Receive, Nurture, Create, and Connect."*

The Oracle's Logic: When you ask a question about the future, you are asking: *"Will energy flow successfully in this direction?"* The breath gives you the immediate status report.

- If the breath is **Purna** (Flowing/Full), the energy pathway is **Open**. The answer is likely YES.
- If the breath is **Shunya** (Blocked/Empty), the energy pathway is **Closed**. The answer is likely NO.

It is that simple. And that brutal. The breath does not lie to spare your feelings. It tells you exactly where the energy is going.

Part Ii: The Myth Of Balance – The 100% Lie

Most beginners fail at Swara divination because they are looking for a "100% Block." They think: *"Well, I can breathe through both sides, so I must be in the middle."*

Wrong. Unless you are in the 2-minute window of the **Sushumna** (The Void), you are **never** balanced. The nasal cycle is a sine wave. It is always tipping. It might be 60/40. It might be 55/45. It might be 51/49.

The Oracle demands Precision. In a 51/49 split, the 51 side is the **Purna** (Full) side. The 49 side is the **Shunya** (Empty) side. Even a 1% difference determines the winner. In a horse race, the horse that wins by a nose still wins the millions. In Swara, the nostril that wins by a millimeter determines the destiny.

The Danger of "Roughly Equal": If you cannot detect the dominant side, you are flying blind. If you guess, you are gambling. This is why we spent time in Book 1 on the "Tests" (Mirror, Finger, etc.). But for divination, we need to go deeper. We need **Instant Detection.** You cannot pull out a mirror in the middle of a business meeting. You need to be able to feel the flow **from the inside**.

Part Iii: The Flow Audit – Advanced Detection Protocols

We are going to upgrade your sensor array. We need methods that are invisible, instant, and infallible.

Protocol 1: The "Flare" Test (Muscular Confirmation)

This is a somatic hack. The dominant nostril is connected to the active brain hemisphere, which increases muscle tone on the *opposite* side of the body, but also increases **micro-control** on the *same* side of the face.

The Test: Without using your hands, try to **flare** your nostrils. Widen them as much as possible. Now, try to twitch just the **Right** one. Then just the **Left** one. You will find that the **Dominant Nostril** feels "stiffer," "wider," and easier to control. The **Blocked Nostril** feels "dead," "flaccid," or harder to twitch.

- **Why it works:** The active turbinate is engorged with blood (erectile tissue). It has higher internal pressure. The blocked side is drained and collapsed. The "Full" side literally feels fuller.

Protocol 2: The "Sniff-Pulse" (Auditory Confirmation)

This is for noisy environments where you can't hear the subtle "roar."

The Test: Take a sharp, short, sudden inhale (like a sniff). Don't do a long draw. Just a quick *sniff-sniff*. Feel the friction point.

- **The Active Side:** The air hits the "roof" of the sinus cavity instantly. It feels sharp and high.
- **The Passive Side:** The air feels like it hits a wall or drags along the bottom. It feels dull and low.
- **The Sound:** The Active side makes a higher-pitched, cleaner sound. The Passive side makes a muffled, lower sound.

Protocol 3: The "Visual Field" Check (Neurological Confirmation)

This is the most advanced, but also the coolest. The nasal cycle is linked to **Hemispheric Lateralization.**

- Right Nostril = Left Brain (Focal Vision).
- Left Nostril = Right Brain (Peripheral Vision).

The Test: Close one eye. Look at an object. Then switch. Which eye feels sharper? Which eye feels brighter?

- If the **Right Eye** feels dominant/brighter -> **Left Nostril** (Moon) is likely active. (Cross-wiring).
- If the **Left Eye** feels dominant/brighter -> **Right Nostril** (Sun) is likely active.
- **Wait, isn't it contralateral?** Yes. But vision is tricky. The *optic nerve* crosses, but the visual *field* is processed by the opposite hemisphere. Generally, increased visual acuity in the **Right Eye** correlates with **Left Brain** activity (Right Nostril), and vice versa.
- *Correction:* Let's stick to the simplest bio-marker. **Active Right Nostril (Sun)** = **Brighter, Sharper Vision**. (Pupils dilate slightly due to Sympathetic activation). **Active Left Nostril (Moon)** = **Softer, Dimmer Vision**. (Pupils constrict slightly). Look at the room. Does it look "High Definition" (Sun) or "Soft Focus" (Moon)?

Part Iv: The Golden Rule – Purna (Full) Vs. Shunya (Empty)

Now that you can identify the side, we establish the **Binary Code**. This is the foundation of every prediction you will make in Book 2.

The Concept of Purna (The Full Side)

- **Sanskrit:** *Purna* (Full, Complete, Whole).
- **The Breath:** The nostril that is flowing openly.

- **The Energy:** This is the "Live Wire." Prana is flowing here.
- **The Meaning:** Success, Life, Growth, Presence, Power, "Yes."
- **The Metaphor:** The Open Door.

The Concept of Shunya (The Empty Side)

- **Sanskrit:** *Shunya* (Empty, Zero, Void).
- **The Breath:** The nostril that is blocked or flowing weakly.
- **The Energy:** This is the "Dead Wire." Prana is absent here.
- **The Meaning:** Failure, Death, Loss, Absence, Weakness, "No."
- **The Metaphor:** The Closed Wall.

The Oracle's First Law:

> *"Energy follows the Breath. If you engage the world through the Full Side, you succeed. If you engage the world through the Empty Side, you fail."*

This sounds abstract. Let's make it concrete. Imagine you are a plug. The Universe is a socket. If you plug into the **Purna** side, the light turns on. If you plug into the **Shunya** side, nothing happens.

Scenario: You want to ask for a raise.

- **Option A:** You walk into your boss's office. Your **Right Nostril** is flowing (Purna). You stand on his Right side (projecting your Full side). You speak.
  - *Result:* Your energy lands. He hears you. The connection is made. **Success is likely.**
- **Option B:** You walk in. Your **Right Nostril** is flowing. But you stand on his *Left* side (projecting your Empty/Shunya side toward him).
  - *Result:* Your words sound hollow. He gets distracted. The energy dissipates into the void. **Failure is likely.**

This is the secret. It is not just about *your* state. It is about **Directional Alignment**. (We will cover this deeply in Sub-Chapter 1.2). But for now, memorize this: **Trust the Flow. Fear the Void.**

Part V: The Oracle Calibration – The "Yes/No" Drill

Before we predict stock markets or marriages, we must calibrate the instrument with simple questions. You need to build trust in your own nose.

The Calibration Drill:

Step 1: The Baseline Sit comfortably. Close your eyes. Identify your **Active Nostril**. (Let's say it is **Right/Sun**). Confirm it is Purna (Full). Confirm the Left is Shunya (Empty).

Step 2: The Known Truths (Calibration) Ask a question you *know* the answer to is YES.

- *"Is my name [Your Name]?"*
- check the breath. Does the Right Nostril flare? Does the flow feel smooth?
    - *Expected Result:* The Active Breath should remain steady or strengthen.

Ask a question you *know* the answer to is NO.

- *"Am I a purple elephant?"*
- Check the breath.
- *Expected Result:* You might feel a momentary "hitch" or "stutter" in the Active Breath. Or a subtle shift toward the Blocked side.
    - *Note:* The breath recoils from untruth.

Step 3: The Small Unknowns Ask a low-stakes question about the immediate future.

- *"Will I get a text message in the next 10 minutes?"*
- Check the breath.
    - If the Active Nostril flows **smoothly and strongly**:

    YES.
    - If the Active Nostril feels **weak, interrupted, or tries to switch: NO.**
- Wait 10 minutes. Verify the result.

The Learning Curve: You will be wrong at first. Not because the breath is wrong, but because your *interpretation* of the signal is noisy. You might mistake a "Hopeful Inhale" for a "Purna Flow." You must learn to detach from the outcome. The Oracle only works if the Operator is neutral.

Part Vi: The "Sushumna" Hazard – The Non-Answer

What if you ask a question and the breath is equal? What if it's the **Sandhi** (The Crossover)?

The Oracle Says: NULL. The computer has crashed. The universe is saying: *"Result Undetermined,"* or *"Not Fate's Business."* Or worse: *"Disaster."*

In **Prashna**, the Sushumna is the **Destroyer**. If you ask: *"Will this business succeed?"* and you are in the Void... The answer is: *"It will consume you, destroy your ego, and yield zero profit. But you might get enlightened."* (Which, for a business, is a **NO**).

The Rule: Never divine in the Void. If you check your nose and it's balanced, stop. Don't interpret. Don't guess. Wait 10 minutes for the Sun or Moon to rise. Only duality can answer questions about duality.

Part Vii: The Compass Of The Nostrils – Ida Vs. Pingala

Not all "Yes" answers are the same. The **Right Nostril (Sun)** says "Yes" differently than the **Left Nostril (Moon).**

- **Pingala (Sun) says YES to:**
  - War, Lawsuits, Debates, Logic, Math, Sex, Eating, Destruction, Speed.
  - *The Vibe:* "Yes, you will crush it."
- **Ida (Moon) says YES to:**
  - Love, Marriage, Friendship, Healing, Arts, Travel, Purchase of Jewelry/Home.
  - *The Vibe:* "Yes, it will flow nicely."

The Cross-Over Error: This is where novices fail.

- **Question:** *"Will I win this lawsuit?"*
- **Breath: Left Nostril (Moon)** is flowing strongly.
- **Novice Interpretation:** "Flow is strong! The answer is Yes!"
- **Master Interpretation:** "Wait. Lawsuits are Solar (War). The Moon is active. This is a mismatch. The Moon says 'Peace/Compromise.' So, will I 'win'? No. I will probably settle or the case will be delayed. It's a 'Soft Yes' at best, or a 'Failure of Intent' at worst."

We will dive deep into this nuance in **Sub-Chapter 1.3**. But for now, remember: **Context Matters.** You want the Breath (Element) to match the Question (Nature).

Part Viii: Summary – The Code Of The Flow

You are now carrying a biological Geiger counter. It detects the radiation of Destiny.

- **Purna (Full Side):** The Live Wire. Success. Presence. Life.
- **Shunya (Empty Side):** The Dead Wire. Failure. Absence. Death.
- **The Test:** Use the Flare, the Sniff, and the Visual Field to

confirm dominance.

- **The Binary:** If the breath flows, the door is open. If the breath is blocked, the door is closed.
- **The Caution:** Beware the Sushumna (Equal Flow). It creates illusions.

Next Step: Now that you can read the *internal* binary (Left vs. Right), we need to map it to the *external* world. Divination is rarely solitary. It usually involves **Another Person**.

- A business partner sitting across the table.
- A lover walking through the door.
- An enemy standing in your path.

Where are they standing relative to your breath? Are they standing in your **Purna** (Full) zone? Or your **Shunya** (Empty) zone? This spatial geometry determines the outcome of the interaction before a word is spoken.

In **Sub-Chapter 1.2**, we unlock the **Geometry of the Question.** We will learn why you should never let a salesperson sit on your empty side. We will learn how to position yourself in a room to guarantee victory. We will learn the secret of the "Front vs. Back" matrix.

Turn the page. The Oracle is about to go 3D.

Author's Note: *We have established the binary code inside the skull (Book 2, Chapter 1.1). Now, we project that code into three-dimensional space. Sub-Chapter 1.2 transforms the abstract concept of "Flow" into a concrete tactical manual for spatial positioning. This is the "Feng Shui of the Body."*

1.2: The Geometry of the Question – The Sniper's Angle

> *"He who places the Messenger on the side of the Flowing Breath obtains the fruit of his desire. He who places the Messenger on the side of the Empty Breath obtains only wind and shadows. O Devi, know that success is not just a matter of Time, but of Place."* — *Shiva Swarodaya*, Verse 68

You are not a static point in the universe. You are a **Vector**. You are a lighthouse sweeping a beam across a dark ocean. Where the beam hits, there is light (Visibility/Success). Where the beam misses, there is darkness (Invisibility/Failure).

In Sub-Chapter 1.1, we learned to identify which bulb is lit inside the lighthouse (Left vs. Right Nostril). In **Sub-Chapter 1.2**, we learn where to aim the beam.

Most people treat space as neutral. They think sitting on the left side of a table is the same as sitting on the right. They think approaching a boss from the front is the same as approaching from the side. They are wrong. **Space is polarized by your breath.**

At any given moment, 50% of the world around you is "Live" (Purna) and 50% is "Dead" (Shunya). If you conduct business in your Dead Zone, you will fail—even if you are smart, prepared, and right. The energy simply won't land. It will fall into the vacuum. If you conduct business in your Live Zone, you can be half-prepared and still win, because the current carries you.

This sub-chapter is about **Geometry**. It is about the "Sniper's Angle." A sniper knows that wind, distance, and angle determine the shot. The **Swara Yogi** knows that the nostril determines the angle of success.

We are going to map the **Matrix of the Room**. We are going to learn why you should never let a salesperson sit on your empty side. We are going to learn how to position your lover to ensure a "Yes." And we are going to learn the terrifying power of the **Shunya Defense**—how to make an enemy powerless simply by standing in their blind spot.

Part I: The Physics Of The Field – The Projected Aura

To understand this, you must stop thinking of the breath as air that stays inside your lungs. Think of the breath as **Pranic Radiation**.

The Beam Analogy: Imagine you have a laser pointer strapped to your nose.

- If your **Right Nostril** is open, the laser is firing out of the right side. It creates a cone of "Charged Space" on your right.
- If your **Left Nostril** is open, the laser is firing out of the left side. It creates a cone of "Charged Space" on your left.

The Law of Connection: For a transaction to happen (a deal, a kiss, a conversation), the other person must be inside the **Laser Cone**. Why? Because the **Purna** (Full) side is where your **Attention**, your **Vitality**, and your **Magnetic Force** are concentrated. The nerves on that side of the body are hyper-sensitized. The aura is denser. The "reception" is 5 bars.

The **Shunya** (Empty) side is where your system is "dormant." The nerves are duller. The aura is thinner. The "reception" is 1 bar or "No Service."

The Tragedy of Misalignment: I see this in corporate boardrooms constantly. A brilliant executive is pitching a million-dollar idea. Her **Right Nostril** (Solar/Logic) is blasting. She is ready to win. But the CEO is sitting on her **Left** (Empty/Lunar) side. She is projecting all her solar power to the Right, but the target is on the Left. The CEO feels "unmoved." He looks at his phone. He interrupts her. She thinks, *"My idea is bad."* No. Her idea is fine.

Her **Geometry** is fatal. She is shouting into the void, while the target sits in the shadows.

Part Ii: The Purna Rule – The Zone Of Life

> *"Let the Messenger, the Questioner, or the Beloved approach from the Filled Side. If they stand in the flow of the breath, they become part of the Yogi's own Prana. Unity is established."*

The Purna Rule is the first law of Swara Geometry. **Purna** means "Full." It refers to the side of the body corresponding to the open nostril.

The Definition:

- If **Right Nostril** is Open -> **Right Side** is Purna.
- If **Left Nostril** is Open -> **Left Side** is Purna.

The Effect: When someone stands in your Purna Zone:

1. **Resonance:** Your nervous system "accepts" them instantly. They feel like an extension of you.
2. **Influence:** Your words land with maximum impact. You are "feeding" them with your Prana.
3. **Success:** The answer to any question asked in this zone is biased toward **YES**. (Growth/Agreement).

The Protocol for "Yes": If you want a positive outcome, you must **Enclose the Target**. You must maneuver your body so that the target falls into your Purna Zone.

- **Scenario:** You are asking your boss for a raise.
- **Audit:** Check your nose. **Right Nostril (Sun)** is flowing.
- **The Move:** Walk into the office. Do *not* sit in the chair directly opposite (neutral). Do *not* sit to his right (which puts him on your left/empty side). Stand or sit so that he is to your **Right**. Force him into your Solar beam.

- **The Result:** You speak from the Sun. He receives the Sun. The energy is direct. His resistance melts because he is biologically coupled to your active flow.

The "Feeding" Metaphor: Think of the Purna breath as a garden hose. If you want to water a plant (the deal), you point the hose at it. If you point the hose (Right Nostril) away from the plant (Target on Left), the plant dries up. **Always water the target.**

Part Iii: The Shunya Rule – The Zone Of Death

> *"If the Messenger stands on the Empty Side, the message is hollow. If the Warrior attacks from the Empty Side, the Yogi is vulnerable. Treat the Shunya side as a cliff—whatever falls there is lost."*

The Shunya Rule is the law of negation. **Shunya** means "Empty" or "Void." It refers to the side of the body corresponding to the blocked/passive nostril.

The Definition:

- If **Right Nostril** is Open -> **Left Side** is Shunya.
- If **Left Nostril** is Open -> **Right Side** is Shunya.

The Effect: When someone stands in your Shunya Zone:

1. **Dissonance:** Your nervous system "rejects" or "ignores" them. They feel like an annoyance or a ghost.
2. **Drain:** Interacting with them feels exhausting because you have to "reach across" your own midline to pay attention.
3. **Failure:** The answer to any question asked in this zone is biased toward **NO.** (Rejection/Loss).

The Protocol for "No": This is the secret weapon of the Swara Yogi. Sometimes, you *want* to fail. You want to reject a salesperson. You want to shut down a toxic relative. You want to end a boring conversation. Do not use words. Use Geometry.

- **Scenario:** A pushy salesperson approaches you.
- **Audit:** Check your nose. **Left Nostril (Moon)** is flowing.
- **The Move:** Pivot your body so he is on your **Right** (Shunya/ Empty side).
- **The Result:** He starts talking. You nod blankly. You do not engage. He feels the "cold shoulder" biologically. He loses his momentum. He walks away. You have "Voided" him.

The "Black Hole" Metaphor: Think of the Shunya side as a black hole. It absorbs light but reflects nothing back. If you put a problem in the black hole, it disappears. But be careful—if you put a *solution* or a *friend* in the black hole, they might disappear too.

Part Iv: The Matrix Of Direction – Front, Back, Top, Bottom

The world is 3D. It's not just Left vs. Right. The *Shiva Swarodaya* provides a sophisticated matrix for directional alignment.

1. The Frontal Cone (Active + Front) = THE WINNING ZONE

- **Geometry:** The target is on your Active Side AND slightly in front of you.
- **Meaning:** Confrontation, Connection, Victory.
- **Outcome: 100% Impact.**
- **Use Case:** Closing a sale, Kissing a lover, Winning a debate.
- **Why:** Our eyes face forward. Our breath shoots forward. This is the zone of maximum conscious projection.

2. The Dorsal Shadow (Active + Back) = THE DANGER ZONE

- **Geometry:** The target is on your Active Side but *behind* you.
- **Meaning:** Betrayal, Hidden Support, or Unseen Threat.
- **Outcome: 50% Impact (Unstable).**
- **Use Case:** Do not use this for business. This is the position

of a "backstabber" or a "shadow advisor."

- **Why:** Even though they are on the Purna side, they are out of your sight. Prana flows, but Awareness is blind. This creates vulnerability.

3. The Empty Front (Passive + Front) = THE RESISTANCE ZONE

- **Geometry:** The target is on your Passive Side but in front of you.
- **Meaning:** Struggle, Negotiation, Effort.
- **Outcome: 25% Impact (Hard Work).**
- **Use Case:** Dealing with difficult tasks that require patience. You have to "drag" the energy across the midline. It works, but it costs double the fuel.

4. The Empty Void (Passive + Back) = THE DEAD ZONE

- **Geometry:** The target is on your Passive Side and behind you.
- **Meaning:** Total Loss, Theft, Irrelevance.
- **Outcome: 0% Impact.**
- **Use Case:** Where you put things you want to forget.
- **Warning:** Never let an enemy stand here. They are invisible to your energy, meaning they can strike without you sensing it.

5. The Vertical Axis (Top vs. Bottom)

- **The Rule:** Prana flows *down* from the head (Heaven) to the feet (Earth).
- **Superiority:** The person who is physically higher (standing vs. sitting, or sitting on a dais) has a **Gravitational Prana Advantage**.
- **The Hack:** If you are in a weak position (Shunya breath), stand up. Changing your verticality disrupts the static field. Never negotiate a salary while sitting in a low chair looking up at your boss. You are fighting Gravity and Geometry. Stand up, or raise your chair.

Part V: Strategic Seating – The Boardroom Hack

Let's apply this to the most common modern battlefield: **The Meeting Table.**

The Setup: You enter a conference room. Rectangular table. 6 chairs. Where do you sit? Most people choose based on "social hierarchy" (head of the table) or "hiding" (back of the room). The Swara Yogi chooses based on **Nostril Dominance.**

Step 1: The Audit Before entering, check the nose.

- **Status: Right Nostril (Sun)** is blasting.
- **Goal:** I need to convince the Key Decision Maker (KDM).

Step 2: The Map You need the KDM to be on your **Right Side** (Purna).

- If you sit at the head of the table, the KDM must be on your right.
- If you sit on the side, ensure the KDM is to your right.

Step 3: The "Trap" What if you sit down, and the breath *switches* halfway through the meeting? (This happens. Ultradian rhythms cycle). Suddenly, your Right side becomes Shunya. The KDM is now in the Dead Zone. You will feel the connection drop. The KDM will start looking at his watch.

The Executive Pivot: You must re-align the geometry.

- **Option A (Physical Move):** Stand up. Walk to the whiteboard. By moving to the front of the room, you can reposition yourself so the KDM is on your new Active Side (Left).
- **Option B (Body Torque):** Turn your chair. Angle your body so that you are "facing" the KDM with the new Active Side.
- **Option C (The Override):** Use the **Fist Hack** (Chapter 5, Book 1) under the table to force the breath back to the Right.

Writer's Confession: I once won a consulting contract simply because I kept moving my chair. The client asked, "Why do you keep shifting?" I said, "I think better from this angle." I was actually chasing him with my Purna breath. Every time my nostril twitched, I adjusted the angle to keep him in the beam. He signed. He said, "I feel like you really *get* me." He didn't know he was being bathed in a Solar laser.

Part Vi: The Lover's Approach – Tantric Geometry

Divination is not just for business. It is for **Love**. *Prashna* (Question) also applies to: *"Will she say yes?"*

The *Shiva Swarodaya* gives explicit instructions on **Sexual and Romantic Approach**. The geometry of seduction is delicate.

The Rule of the Receiver: In romance, you are usually asking for *receptivity*. Therefore, the **Moon (Left)** is generally the preferred channel for love.

Scenario: You want to ask someone out, or initiate intimacy.

- **Audit:** Ensure your **Left Nostril (Moon)** is flowing. (This activates Right Brain empathy/connection).
- **The Position:** Approach them from their **Left Side**.
    - *Wait, why their Left?*
    - Because if *your* Left is flowing, you want to resonate with *their* Left.
    - Ideally, you want a **Mirror Flow** (Lunar to Lunar) for deep connection.
    - Or a **Complementary Flow** (Solar to Lunar) for passion.

The "Heart-Side" Logic: The heart is on the left. Approaching from the Left allows the "Lunar" (Female/Receptive) energies to mingle. Approaching a lover from the Right (Solar/Male) while breathing Solar can feel aggressive or transactional. Unless you want "Rough Sex" (Solar), stick to the Left for romance.

The Kissing Test: Have you ever noticed that when you kiss, you naturally tilt your head one way? Science says 2/3 of people tilt to the right. Swara Yoga says: **You tilt toward the Open Nostril.** You are unconsciously trying to align the Purna side with the partner to maximize the sensory intake of the kiss. Next time you kiss, check your nose. You will be amazed.

Part Vii: The Warrior's Stance – The Shunya Defense

> *"When the enemy attacks with a sword, keep him on the Closed Side. His strikes will miss. His anger will fade. He will be like a man fighting fog."*

This is the martial application. In a physical fight (or a heated argument), you want to protect your core. Your **Purna (Full)** side is your "Open Door." It is where you are vulnerable to entry. Your **Shunya (Empty)** side is your "Closed Wall."

The Defensive Protocol: If someone is screaming at you, or threatening you:

1. **Check the Nose: Right Nostril** is open.
2. **The Pivot:** Turn your body so your **Left Side** (Shunya) is facing them.
3. **The Effect:**

- **Energetically:** You are giving them "nothing." You are not receiving their anger. You are not feeding their fire.
- **Psychologically:** You feel detached. Their insults don't "land."
- **Magically:** The text claims their aggression will dissipate because it finds no purchase.

The "Wolf" Technique: The text mentions that if a dog (or wolf/

tiger) attacks, you should keep it on your Empty Side. I have tested this with aggressive stray dogs in India. (Disclaimer: Be careful). When a barking dog approaches, if you face it with your Purna (Full) side, it senses your Prana/Fear/Engagement. It escalates. If you turn your Shunya (Empty) side to it and ignore it, the dog often gets confused. It senses a "void." It loses interest and walks away. You have become energetically invisible.

Part Viii: The Somatic Lab – The Resistance Test

We need to prove that your Purna side is stronger than your Shunya side. This is a demonstration you can do with a friend.

Exercise: The Lateral Push Test

Step 1: Calibration Check your nose. Identify the Active Nostril. (e.g., Right/Sun is active). This means **Right Arm** is Purna, **Left Arm** is Shunya.

Step 2: The Purna Test

- Stand straight. Extend your **Right Arm** (Active side) out to the side, parallel to the floor.
- Ask your friend to try to push your arm down.
- Resist with full strength.
- **Observation:** You should feel solid, locked in. The arm stays up easily.

Step 3: The Shunya Test

- Now extend your **Left Arm** (Passive side) out to the side.
- Ask your friend to push it down with the *same* force.
- Resist with full strength.
- **Observation:** You will likely be weaker. The arm will buckle or drop faster. You will feel like you have less "leverage."

The Takeaway: Your structure is physically compromised on the Empty side. Imagine negotiating a deal with your "Weak Arm" forward. Imagine fighting a war with your "Weak Side" exposed. **Always put your Strong Side forward.**

Part Ix: The Case Study – The Billion Dollar Handshake

I want to close with a story about a merger that failed. Two CEOs met to sign a historic deal. CEO A (The Buyer) was a Swara practitioner. CEO B (The Seller) was not.

They met on a stage for a photo op and the handshake. CEO A checked his breath: **Left Nostril (Moon)** was active. He intuitively positioned himself to the **Left** of CEO B. This put CEO B in his **Purna Zone**. CEO A felt great. He felt connected, powerful, and ready.

But CEO B? We don't know his breath, but we know the result. CEO B felt "off." In the photos, he looks uncomfortable. He is leaning away. Just before signing, CEO B hesitated. "I need to review the terms one last time," he said. The signing was delayed. That night, news broke of a scandal in CEO A's company. The deal collapsed.

The Analysis: Why did CEO B hesitate? Perhaps he was intuitive. Perhaps he felt CEO A "feeding" on him (Purna dominance). Or perhaps the geometry was simply wrong for a "merger" (Union). In a merger, you want **Equal Geometry**. Side-by-side can be tricky if one person is Purna and the other is Shunya. The best geometry for a merger? **Face to Face.** Eyes to Eyes. Breath to Breath. Or, wait for the **Sushumna** (if you want spiritual union) or the **Earth Element** (if you want stability).

This brings us to the next layer of complexity. Binary (Left/Right) is powerful. But it is not enough. The breath has more than just "Side." It has **Shape**. It has **Color**. It has **Taste**.

Is your breath a Square (Earth)? A Circle (Air)? A Triangle (Fire)? If you are breathing "Fire" on your Right side, you will burn the deal. If you are breathing "Water" on your Right side, you will flow through the deal.

In **Chapter 2: The Five Elemental Codes**, we leave the binary world. We enter the **Holographic World**. We will learn how to spit on a mirror to see the shape of your destiny. We will learn how to taste the future on your tongue.

Turn the page. The Oracle is about to get High Definition.

1.3: The Polarity of Success – The Quality of the Yes

"The Sun burns the seed to release the energy. The Moon waters the seed to grow the root. If you ask the Sun to grow the root, it will scorch the earth. If you ask the Moon to burn the forest, it will only weep. Success is not just 'Yes'; success is Resonance."

— Shiva Swarodaya, Verse 115

So, you've mastered the Binary.

You ask a question: "Will I win?"

You check your nose. The Right Nostril is flowing strong (Purna).

The Oracle says: YES.

You go out and fight. You survive. But the victory feels hollow. The enemy wasn't destroyed; they just retreated to fight another day. You spent more money than you won.

You come back to the Oracle and scream: "You lied! You said Yes!"

The Oracle did not lie. The energy was flowing. The door was open.

But you tried to walk through a Solar Door wearing Lunar Shoes.

This is the Cross-Over Error.

It is the most common mistake in advanced divination.

We assume that "Success" is a generic commodity. We think a win is a win.

But in the energetic universe, there are two distinct flavors of success:

1. **Solar Success (Pingala):** Conquest, Domination, Speed, Heat, Clarity, Extraction.
2. **Lunar Success (Ida):** Connection, Stability, Growth, Cool-

ness, Integration, Retention.

If you ask a Solar question (e.g., “Will I crush my competition?”) while the Lunar Breath is flowing... the answer might be "Yes" (Flowing), but the quality of the result will be Lunar.

Instead of crushing them, you might merge with them. Or you might forgive them.

You get a result, but it’s not the result you wanted.

In this sub-chapter, we are going to learn Energetic Matching.

We are going to categorize every major human activity into Solar or Lunar buckets.

We are going to dissect the disaster of the "Mismatched Yes."

And we are going to learn the discipline of the Sniper: Don't shoot until the wind matches the bullet.

Part I: The Solar Classification – The Hard Yes

> *“In the flow of the Sun, perform acts of cruelty, courage, and calculation. Buy, sell, eat, and destroy. Do not marry. Do not enter a new home.”*

The Right Nostril (Pingala) is the channel of Mars and Saturn (in its structural aspect). It is the frequency of high-voltage output.

When you receive a "Yes" from the Solar Breath, it is a Hard Yes.

It is sharp, fast, and often irreversible.

The Solar Portfolio (Activities that DEMAND a Right Breath):

1. Warfare & Conflict:
   Lawsuits, physical fights, debates, firing an employee, breaking up with a toxic partner.

Why: You need the Left Brain (Logic) to strategize and the Sympathetic Nervous System (Adrenaline) to execute. A Lunar breath here makes you weak, emotional, and hesitant.

2. Logic & Mathematics:
   Coding, accounting, engineering, complex architectural planning, studying science.
   Why: These are linear tasks. The Solar breath activates the linear processor.
3. Short-Term Travel:
   Driving fast, commuting, sprinting.
   Why: Solar energy is kinetic. It likes speed.
4. Digestion & Eating:
   Consuming heavy meals, drinking alcohol.
   Why: The "Gastric Fire" (Jataragni) is Solar.
5. Sex (The Masculine/Active Pole):
   Penetration, drive, stamina, conception (of a male child, according to ancient texts).
   Why: It requires heat and projection.
6. Sales & Negotiation (The "Closer"):
   Asking for the money. Closing the deal.
   Why: Closing is an act of dominance. You are collapsing the wave function. You are forcing a decision.

The Solar "Yes" Signature:

When the Right Nostril gives you a Yes, it feels like Lightning.

It is exciting, slightly aggressive, and very clear.

There is no "maybe." There is no "let's wait and see."

The energy says: "GO. Take it. It's yours."

Part Ii: The Lunar Classification – The Soft Yes

"In the flow of the Moon, perform acts of stability, healing,

and decoration. Marry, make friends, sow seeds, and enter the sanctuary. Do not go to war. Do not gamble."

The Left Nostril (Ida) is the channel of Venus, Jupiter, and Mercury. It is the frequency of flow, magnetism, and reception.

When you receive a "Yes" from the Lunar Breath, it is a Soft Yes.

It is stable, nurturing, and sticky.

The Lunar Portfolio (Activities that DEMAND a Left Breath):

1. Relationships & Marriage:
   Proposing, wedding ceremonies, making peace, socializing, networking.
   Why: You need the Right Brain (Empathy) to connect. A Solar breath here makes you argumentative and cold.
2. Creation & Art:
   Painting, writing (fiction), music, brainstorming, designing.
   Why: These are non-linear tasks. The Lunar breath opens the "Dream Channel."
3. Long-Term Travel:
   Starting a pilgrimage, moving to a new country.
   Why: The Moon governs "The Path." It offers stamina and protection over long distances.
4. Healing & Medicine:
   Taking medicine, surgery (recovery phase), therapy, resting.
   Why: The Parasympathetic system (Moon) is the only state in which tissue regenerates.
5. Agriculture & Investment:
   Planting seeds, buying land, buying jewelry, saving money.
   Why: The Moon rules "Accumulation." The Sun burns; the Moon gathers. If you want your investment to grow (not just spike and crash), buy it on the Moon.
6. Spirituality (Bhakti/Devotion):
   Prayer, chanting, ritual.

Why: It requires surrender.

The Lunar "Yes" Signature:

When the Left Nostril gives you a Yes, it feels like Water.

It is cool, reassuring, and expansive.

It doesn't scream "Go!" It whispers "Flow."

The energy says: “Allow it. It is coming to you.”

Part Iii: The Cross-Over Error – The Anatomy Of A Mess

Now we get to the danger zone.

What happens when you mix them up?

What happens when you ask a Solar Question but get a Lunar Answer?

Case Study 1: The "Nice" Lawsuit

- **The Question:** *"Will I win this lawsuit against my business partner?"*
- **The Breath: Left Nostril (Moon)** is flowing Purna (Full).
- **The Oracle Interpretation:**
  - *Binary:* Yes (Flow is strong).
  - *Polarity:* Mismatch. (Lawsuit = Solar; Breath = Lunar).
- The Outcome: You win, but...

  Because the energy was Lunar (Connection/Peace), you likely settle out of court. Or you win, but you feel guilty about it. Or you "make peace" in a way that leaves money on the table.

  You didn't crush the enemy (Solar result). You absorbed the enemy (Lunar result).

  If your goal was total domination, this "Yes" is actually a failure.

Case Study 2: The Volatile Marriage

- **The Question:** *"Should I propose to her tonight?"*
- **The Breath: Right Nostril (Sun)** is flowing Purna (Full).
- **The Oracle Interpretation:**
    - *Binary:* Yes (Flow is strong).
    - *Polarity:* Mismatch. (Marriage = Lunar; Breath = Solar).
- The Outcome: She says Yes, but...

  The proposal energy is Solar (Heat/Aggression). The moment is intense, sexual, perhaps impulsive.

  The marriage starts on a "Hot" note.

  The relationship becomes prone to fighting, ego clashes, and dominance struggles. It lacks the cooling stability of the Moon.

  It burns bright and burns out fast.

The Master's Rule:

Alignment > Binary.

A "No" (Blocked Breath) is often better than a "Mismatched Yes."

If I want to sue someone and my Moon is flowing, I do not file the papers. I wait.

I wait for the Sun to rise.

I want the wind at my back, not a crosswind.

Part Iv: The Nuance Of "Weak" Vs. "Strong" Flow

We need to refine our sensors further.

The breath is not just "Open" or "Closed." It has Volume and Velocity.

1. The Torrent (Rapid/Strong)

- *Feel:* Loud, rushing, high pressure.

- *Meaning:* High Intensity. Fast results.
- *Solar Torrent:* Violence, Explosion, Immediate Victory.
- *Lunar Torrent:* Flood of Emotion, Overwhelming Love, Rapid Healing.

2. The Stream (Steady/Calm)

- *Feel:* Silent, smooth, consistent deep breath.
- *Meaning:* Stability. Long-lasting results.
- *Solar Stream:* Consistent work, steady progress, disciplined execution.
- *Lunar Stream:* Deep peace, long marriage, steady growth of wealth.

3. The Trickle (Weak/Erratic)

- *Feel:* The nostril is open, but the air feels "thin" or hesitant.
- Meaning: "Yes, but..."

  The door is open, but there is clutter in the hallway.
  Success will come with delays, caveats, or compromises.
  Advice: If you get a Trickle Yes on a high-stakes question, treat it as a Soft No. It's not strong enough to bet the farm on.

Part V: The Strategic Pause – Waiting For The Turn

This is where Swara Yoga becomes a discipline of patience.
In the West, we are taught: "If you want it, go get it NOW."
In Swara, we say: "If you want it, check the time."
The Sniper's Discipline:
Imagine you are a sniper. You have the target in your sights.
But the wind is blowing Left (Lunar), and you need to shoot Right (Solar).

Do you shoot?

No. You wait.

You breathe. You watch the grass move.

You wait for the Ultradian Shift.

Every 60-90 minutes, the wind changes.

You wait for the Right Nostril to pop open.

Click.

Now the wind matches the shot.

Pull the trigger.

The Real-World Application:

You have a difficult email to send (Solar/Conflict).

You sit down at 10:00 AM.

Check nose: Left (Moon) is flowing.

Action: Do not send. Save as Draft.

Wait. Go get coffee. Do some admin work.

11:15 AM. Check nose. Right (Sun) is flowing.

Action: Re-read the email. (You will likely edit it to be sharper). Send.

This simple act of waiting 75 minutes changes the energetic signature of the email from "Whiny/Emotional" to "Commanding/Effective."

Part Vi: The "Void" Yes – The Ultimate Trap

We touched on this in Chapter 1.1, but we must drill it deeper.

What if the breath is Equal (Sushumna)?

And you ask: "Will I become a millionaire?"

The amateur thinks: "Wow, perfect balance! That must mean huge success!"

The Master knows: Sushumna burns matter.

If you get a "Yes" in the Void, the result is usually **Spiritual Success at the cost of Material Failure.**

- You might lose all your money, but realize money is an illusion. (Great for a monk, terrible for you).
- You might lose the job, but find your soul's purpose.

The "Ghost" Outcome:

Projects started in the Sushumna tend to become "Ghosts."

They hover. They never fully manifest, but they never fully die.

They drain your energy without giving a return.

- *Example:* That screenplay you've been "working on" for 10 years but never finish? You probably conceived it in the Void. It loves the realm of ideas (Ether) but refuses to enter the realm of matter (Earth).

The Protocol:

If you see the Void: Abort.

Do not ask. Do not act.

Close your eyes. Meditate for 5 minutes.

Let the Ghost pass.

Part Vii: Advanced Polarity – The "Question Re-Framing" Hack

Here is a Jedi trick.

Sometimes, you cannot wait. You have to act now.

But the breath is wrong.

- *Situation:* You need to fire someone (Solar).
- *Breath:* Left Nostril (Moon).
- *Constraint:* You have to do it in 5 minutes.

You can't change the breath in time. So, change the question.

Re-frame the activity to match the current breath.

How to Re-Frame:

Instead of viewing the firing as a "Solar Attack" (You are fired!), view it as a "Lunar Separation" (We are setting you free / We are healing the team).

- *Solar Approach:* "Get out, you're incompetent." (Requires Right Breath).
- *Lunar Approach:* "This isn't working for either of us. I want you to be happy, and you aren't happy here. Let's part ways with love." (Requires Left Breath).

The Result:

Because you aligned the style of the action with the flow of the breath, you get a "Purna" result.

The employee leaves.

But instead of a screaming match (failed Solar), it becomes a tearful but peaceful goodbye (successful Lunar).

You achieved the goal (firing him) by surfing the Lunar wave.

The Universal Law:

You can do almost anything on any breath, IF you adjust the style of the action to match the frequency.

- You can have sex on a Lunar breath (Make love, don't f*ck).

- You can negotiate on a Lunar breath (Collaborate, don't dominate).
- You can rest on a Solar breath (Active recovery, stretching, not napping).

Part Viii: Somatic Lab – Tasting The Two Wines

We need to sensitize you to the "flavor" of the two breaths.

This exercise will anchor the feeling of Solar vs. Lunar success in your nervous system.

The Visualization Drill:

Step 1: The Solar Simulation

- Close your eyes. Block your **Left Nostril**. Breathe only through the Right.
- Speed up the breath. Make it loud.
- *Visualize:* You are a General on a horse, looking down at a battlefield. You have a sword. You are about to scream "Charge!"
- *Feel:* The heat in the belly. The tightness in the chest. The laser focus. The desire to *pierce*.
- *Anchor:* This is the **Solar Yes**. It feels like **Steel**.

Step 2: The Lunar Simulation

- Switch. Block the **Right Nostril**. Breathe only through the Left.
- Slow the breath down. Make it silent.
- *Visualize:* You are a Gardener in a lush forest. It is raining gently. You are planting a seed in rich, dark soil.
- *Feel:* The coolness in the forehead. The expansion in the heart. The patience. The desire to *embrace*.
- *Anchor:* This is the **Lunar Yes**. It feels like **Silk**.

Step 3: The Audit

Open your eyes.

Think of the biggest goal in your life right now.

Which feeling does it need? Steel or Silk?

Check your nose.

Does it match?

Part Ix: Summary – The Matrix Of Nuance

We have graduated from "Yes/No."

We are now operating in 4 Dimensions.

BREATH	QUESTION TYPE	RESULT	VERDICT
Right (Sun)	Solar (War/Biz)	**Explosive Success**	**PERFECT**
Left (Moon)	Lunar (Love/Art)	**Deep Success**	**PERFECT**
Right (Sun)	Lunar (Love/Art)	Volatile/Unstable	**MISMATCH (Danger)**
Left (Moon)	Solar (War/Biz)	Weak/Compromised	**MISMATCH (Weakness)**
Void (Center)	Any Material	**Dissolution**	**ABORT**

Conclusion:

The Oracle is not a magic 8-ball. It is a mirror of cosmic mechanics.

If you ask the universe for Fire, make sure your chimney is open (Right Nostril).

If you ask the universe for Rain, make sure your bucket is out (Left Nostril).

But...

What if the "Yes" is complex?

What if the deal involves money (Earth), travel (Air), and conflict (Fire)?

The binary system (Sun/Moon) is great, but it's black and white.

The real world is Technicolor.

The breath has more than just "Side." It has Element.

- Is your breath Square? (Earth)
- Is your breath Crescent? (Water)
- Is your breath Triangular? (Fire)

In Chapter 2: The Five Elemental Codes, we take the magnifying glass to the breath.

We will learn to see the Tattvas.

We will learn why a "Square Breath" guarantees wealth, while a "Circular Breath" guarantees you will lose your keys.

We will learn to spit on a mirror to see the shape of God.

Turn the page. The Oracle is about to show you the elemental fabric of reality.

CHAPTER 2: THE FIVE ELEMENTAL CODES (DECODING THE TATTVAS)

2.1: The Mirror of Truth – Shape and Length

> *"The breath has a shape, a color, and a length. It is not merely air; it is the ink with which the Universe writes your destiny. If you can read the ink before it dries, you can re-write the script." — Shiva Swarodaya,* Verse 165

You are living in a pixelated reality. When you look at a computer screen, you see an image. A face, a landscape, a chart. But if you zoom in—deep, deep in—you realize the image is an illusion. It is made of millions of tiny dots. Red, Green, and Blue pixels. The arrangement of these pixels determines whether you see a tragedy or a comedy.

The ancient Tantrics understood this 5,000 years before Silicon Valley invented the screen. They realized that "Reality" is not solid. It is made of five fundamental building blocks called **Tattvas** (Elements).

- **Earth (Prithvi):** The Solid Pixel (Stability).
- **Water (Jala):** The Fluid Pixel (Connection).
- **Fire (Agni):** The Radiant Pixel (Transformation).
- **Air (Vayu):** The Kinetic Pixel (Movement).
- **Ether (Akasha):** The Empty Pixel (Space).

Here is the secret that physics is only just beginning to rediscover: **You are projecting these pixels.** Every time you exhale, you are not just releasing carbon dioxide. You are projecting a holographic grid of Tattvas into the world.

- If you exhale **Earth**, you project stability. Deals close. Buildings stand.
- If you exhale **Fire**, you project destruction. Arguments explode. Accidents happen.
- If you exhale **Air**, you project chaos. Keys get lost. Minds wander.

In Book 1, we learned to check if the computer was "On" (Right/ Left Nostril). In **Book 2, Chapter 2**, we learn to check **what program is running**. It is not enough to know the Right Nostril (Sun) is active. You need to know: Is it a *Burning* Sun (Fire)? Or a *Stable* Sun (Earth)? One burns the house down. The other builds a solar farm. The difference is the **Element.**

In this sub-chapter, we are going to learn the forensic art of **Tattva Bodha** (Knowledge of Elements). We are going to learn to measure the length of your breath with your fingers. We are going to learn to spit on a mirror (literally) to see the shape of your fate. And you will realize that the future is not a mystery. It is a shape floating in the vapor of your own breath.

Part I: The Physics Of The Tattvas – The 5-Dimensional Breath

Most people think "Earth, Water, Fire" are metaphors. They are not metaphors. They are **Frequency States.**

- **Earth** is a slow, dense vibration. It creates squares, cubes, and heavy matter.
- **Water** is a flowing vibration. It creates curves, waves, and liquids.
- **Fire** is a rapid, ascending vibration. It creates spikes, triangles, and heat.
- **Air** is an erratic, dispersing vibration. It creates circles, spirals, and gas.
- **Ether** is the background field. It has no shape, or infinite shape.

The Breath as the Carrier Signal Your breath is the carrier wave for these frequencies. Depending on your mental state, your digestion, the planetary transits, and the time of day, your breath physically changes its **Shape** and **Flow Geometry**. You cannot see it with the naked eye (unless you are a high-level clairvoyant), but you can measure it physically.

The Oracle's Second Law:

> *"The Nostril determines the Polarity (Yes/No). The Element determines the Result (Good/Bad/Fast/Slow)."*

Example: You ask: *"Will I get rich?"*

- **Nostril:** Right (Sun). -> **YES** (Power).
- **Element:** Fire (Triangle). -> **Result:** You will get rich through aggressive conflict, but you might burn out or get sued.
- **Element:** Earth (Square). -> **Result:** You will get rich slowly, steadily, and keep the money forever.

Same Nostril. Different Fate. The Element is the detail in the contract.

Part Ii: The Forensic Ruler – Measuring Breath Length (Angulas)

> *"The length of the breath reveals the lifespan and the outcome. In Earth, it moves 12 fingers. In Water, 16. In Fire, 4. In Air, 8. In Ether, it flows within."*

The first way to identify the Element is by **Length**. The breath has a "throw distance." When you exhale normally, the air travels a certain distance from the nose before it dissipates. The ancient unit of measurement is the **Angula** (Finger-breadth).

How to Measure (The Finger Test Protocol):

1. **Calibration:** Sit upright. Relax. Hold your hand horizontally under your nose. One "Angula" is roughly the width of your finger. 4 Angulas is roughly the width of your palm (minus the thumb).

2. **The Detect:** Exhale normally (do not blow). Move your hand away from the nose until you can *no longer feel* the air current. Measure the distance from the nostrils to that "vanishing point."

The Decoding Matrix:

1. The Earth Breath (12 Angulas) – The Standard

- **Distance:** Roughly 8–12 fingers (about 6–9 inches).
- **Feel:** It feels steady, heavy, and stops at a "sensible" distance.
- **Meaning:** This is the baseline of health. If you ask a question and the breath is at 12 Angulas, the result is **Stable**.
    - *Prediction:* "It will happen as expected."

2. The Water Breath (16 Angulas) – The Projection

- **Distance:** Roughly 16 fingers (about 12 inches). It projects far down.
- **Feel:** It feels like a long, cool stream pouring down. It is "heavy" air.
- **Meaning:** Expansion, flow, connection.
    - *Prediction:* "The result will be greater than expected. There is gain. Travel is likely."
    - *Note:* Water flows *down*. The sensation is a downward current.

3. The Fire Breath (4 Angulas) – The Spike

- **Distance:** Very short. Roughly 4 fingers (3 inches).
- **Feel:** It is short, sharp, and hot. It tends to curl *upward* toward the bridge of the nose.
- **Meaning:** Intensity, concentration, destruction.
    - *Prediction:* "The result will be fast and violent. Conflict is certain. Obstacles will be burned, or you will be burned."
    - *Note:* Fire flows *up*. The sensation is heat hitting the upper lip.

4. The Air Breath (8 Angulas) – The Scatter

- **Distance:** Variable (8 fingers). But the key is **Direction.**
- **Feel:** It feels slanted. It does not flow straight down. It flows to the side. It is erratic.
- **Meaning:** Instability, movement, anxiety.
  - *Prediction:* "The result is unsure. Minds will change. The target is moving."

5. The Ether Breath (Zero Angulas) – The Void

- **Distance:** You cannot feel it outside the nose.
- **Feel:** The breath seems to dissolve inside the nostrils.
- **Meaning:** Death, Spiritual absorption, Zero result.
  - *Prediction:* "Nothing will happen."

Part Iii: The Mirror Test (Chhaya Prasna) – Seeing The Shape

Measuring length requires sensitivity. Seeing shapes requires only a mirror. This is the most famous technique in the *Shiva Swarodaya*, known as **Chhaya Prasna** (Shadow Questioning). It relies on the physics of condensation vapor. The "spin" of the breath creates a geometric pattern on the glass.

The Protocol:

1. **The Tool:** A clean, cool mirror. (Or a polished phone screen).
2. **The Distance:** Hold it very close (1 inch) under the nostrils.
3. **The Action:** Exhale steadily and smoothly onto the glass. **Do not blow hard.** Just release the air.
4. **The Read:** Immediately look at the shape of the fog patch before it evaporates.

The Shape Decoder:

1. The Square (Earth / Prithvi)

- **Visual:** The condensation forms a blocky, rectangular, or square shape. It looks dense and spreads evenly.
- **The Code: Stability.**
- **The Oracle:**
    - *Financial Question:* "Yes. Solid gain. Real estate, gold, long-term stocks."
    - *Relationship:* "Yes. Marriage, commitment, boring but safe."
    - *Health:* "Recovery is slow but permanent."
    - *Strategy:* **Hold.** Do not change the plan. Build upon it.

2. The Crescent / Half-Moon (Water / Jala)

- **Visual:** The condensation forms a curved shape, like a smile or a crescent moon.
- **The Code: Flow & Gain.**
- **The Oracle:**
    - *Financial Question:* "Yes. Quick cash flow. Liquid assets. A windfall."
    - *Relationship:* "Yes. Deep romance, sex, fluidity, pregnancy."
    - *Health:* "Healing is fast."
    - *Strategy:* **Move.** Connect. Travel. (Water loves movement).

3. The Triangle (Fire / Agni)

- **Visual:** The condensation forms a shape with a peak pointing upward (towards the nose) or a jagged, sharp patch.
- **The Code: Transformation & Conflict.**
- **The Oracle:**
    - *Financial Question:* "High risk. You might win big or lose big. Gambling energy."
    - *Relationship:* "Arguments. Passion. But likely a breakup or a fight."
    - *Health:* "Fever, surgery, acute inflammation."

  - *Strategy:* **Attack.** Or Cut. If you need to fire someone, wait for the Triangle. If you want peace, avoid the Triangle.

4. The Circle / Oval (Air / Vayu)

- **Visual:** The condensation forms a round, diffuse, or oval shape. It fades very quickly.
- **The Code: Instability & Movement.**
- **The Oracle:**
  - *Financial Question:* "Money comes and goes. Losses likely. Fraud."
  - *Relationship:* "Fickle. They are cheating or leaving. No commitment."
  - *Health:* "Nervous disorders, anxiety, trembling."
  - *Strategy:* **Run.** Escape. This is the element of "running away." If you want to leave a bad situation, wait for the Circle.

5. The Scattered Dots (Ether / Akasha)

- **Visual:** No cohesive shape. Just tiny droplets scattered like stars. Or a very faint mist that vanishes instantly.
- **The Code: Void.**
- **The Oracle:**
  - *All Questions:* **NO.**
  - *Meaning:* The energy has not formed into matter. It remains in the unmanifest.
  - *Strategy:* **Pray.** Meditate. Do not act.

Part Iv: The Elemental Profiles – Deep Dive Interpretation

Knowing the shape is step one. Knowing the **Soul** of the shape is step two. You need to understand the personality of the Tattva to give a nuanced reading.

1. EARTH (The Banker)

- **Vibe:** Slow, heavy, reliable, stubborn.
- **Best For:** Buying a house, starting a construction project, signing a 30-year contract, fixing a broken bone.
- **Worst For:** Sprinting, quick trades, artistic improvisation.
- **Case Study:** A client asked, *"Will this startup succeed?"* He exhaled a **Square**. *Interpretation:* "It will not be a 'Unicorn' (fast growth). It will be a slow, boring, profitable business that lasts 20 years. Don't expect a quick exit." (He was disappointed, wanted fast cash. But 5 years later, he owns a steady logistics firm. The Oracle was right).

2. WATER (The Lover)

- **Vibe:** Fluid, emotional, adaptive, persuasive.
- **Best For:** Sex, marriage proposals, poetry, buying clothes, travel by sea, healing ceremonies.
- **Worst For:** Setting boundaries, strict discipline, warfare.
- **Case Study:** A woman asked, *"Is he cheating?"* She exhaled a **Crescent (Water)**. *Interpretation:* Water binds. It flows together. It is the element of "mixing." "No, he is not leaving. In fact, he is deeply emotionally attached. But Water is fluid—he might be 'flirting' (flow), but the bond is with you." (Turns out, he was planning a surprise vacation).

3. FIRE (The General)

- **Vibe:** Hot, sharp, cruel, illuminated.
- **Best For:** Litigation, debating, eating, sex (aggressive), killing pests/viruses, surgery.
- **Worst For:** Peacemaking, gardening, sleeping.
- **Case Study:** A lawyer asked, *"Will I win the case?"* He exhaled a **Triangle (Fire)**. *Interpretation:* "Yes. But it will be ugly. You will destroy the witness. You will burn bridges. Victory is certain, but there will be casualties." (He won, but the op-

posing counsel filed a grievance against him for aggression. Victory with a cost).

4. AIR (The Thief)

- **Vibe:** Fast, dry, lying, moving.
- **Best For:** Running away, stealing (literally, the texts say Air is good for theft), changing jobs, flying.
- **Worst For:** Anything requiring trust.
- **Case Study:** A man asked, *"Should I lend my brother money?"* He exhaled a **Circle (Air)**. *Interpretation:* "Air moves away. It does not return. If you lend it, consider it a gift. It will blow away like the wind."

5. ETHER (The Monk)

- **Vibe:** Silent, empty, vast.
- **Best For:** Dying, Samadhi, renouncing the world.
- **Worst For:** Living.

Part V: The Somatic Lab – Calibrating Your Tattvas

You cannot just read about this. You must calibrate your instrument. You need to see your own breath.

Exercise: The Mirror Audit

Materials: A small hand mirror. A quiet room. **Time:** 10 minutes.

Step 1: Baseline Sit comfortably. Close your eyes. Visualize a **Yellow Square** (Earth) at the base of your spine. Chant the seed sound *LAM* internally. Feel heavy. Open your eyes. Bring the mirror up. Exhale. *Look:* Do you see the Square? Or at least a dense, rectangular patch?

Step 2: The Shift Close your eyes. Visualize a **Red Triangle** (Fire) at your navel. Chant *RAM*. Feel hot. Feel angry. Open eyes. Mirror up. Exhale. *Look:* Did the shape change? Did it become spikier? Smaller?

Step 3: The Observation For the next 24 hours, keep the mirror in your pocket. Every time you have a strong emotion, check the mirror.

- When you are hungry: You will likely see **Fire**.
- When you are sleepy: You will likely see **Earth**.
- When you are crying: You will likely see **Water**.
- When you are anxious: You will likely see **Air**.

The Realization: You are not a fixed solid. You are a shifting cloud of elements. Divination is simply checking the weather report of your soul.

Part VI: The "Compound Element" – Advanced Forensics

Real life is messy. Sometimes you see a "Square with a tail." Or a "Triangle inside a Circle." This is **Compound Elements**. Just as you can have "Red-Orange," you can have "Fire-Air."

How to Read Hybrids:

- **Dominant Shape:** The main body of the vapor. (This is the Primary Outcome).
- **Secondary Shape:** The edges or distortions. (This is the Modifier).
- **Example:** A Square (Earth) with jagged edges (Fire).
    - *Reading:* "Stable success (Earth), but achieved through conflict (Fire)."
    - *Translation:* You will get the house, but you will fight the bank for it.
- **Example:** A Crescent (Water) that evaporates instantly (Air).
    - *Reading:* "Emotional gain (Water) that is fleeting (Air)."
    - *Translation:* A passionate weekend fling that ends on

Monday.

The Master's Eye: Don't get bogged down in geometry class. Use the **Vibe**. Does the patch look "Solid" or "Flimsy"? Does it look "Sharp" or "Soft"? Trust your intuition. The mirror is just a prop to focus your psychic vision.

Conclusion: The Hologram is Revealed

You now possess a technology that makes smartphones look like stone tools. You can measure the invisible pixels of reality. You can look at a vapor patch on a piece of glass and know if you will become a millionaire or a monk.

- **Earth (Square/12 fingers):** The rock. Bet on it.
- **Water (Crescent/16 fingers):** The river. Flow with it.
- **Fire (Triangle/4 fingers):** The sword. Wield it.
- **Air (Circle/8 fingers):** The wind. Watch it.
- **Ether (Dots/0 fingers):** The ghost. Fear it.

But... What if you don't have a mirror? What if you are in the dark? What if you need to be even more subtle?

The Elements don't just have shapes. They have **Tastes**. Yes, literally. When the Fire element is active, your mouth tastes bitter/hot. When the Earth element is active, your mouth tastes sweet.

In **Sub-Chapter 2.2**, we are going to learn **The Taste of Time**. We are going to learn how to stick out your tongue and taste the future. We are going to learn why anxiety tastes like metal, and success tastes like honey.

Turn the page. The banquet is served.

2.2: The Taste of Time – Sensory Identification

> "The Universe has a flavor. When Earth rules, the mouth is sweet. When Fire rules, the mouth is bitter. He who knows the taste of the Tattvas need not ask the stars; he simply swallows his own nectar and knows the truth."
>
> — Shiva Swarodaya, Verses 170-175

Have you ever walked into a room and felt a "bad taste in your mouth"?

Have you ever met someone and felt that the interaction was "sweet"?

Have you ever been in a crisis where the situation felt "sour"?

We use these words as metaphors. But in Swara Yoga, metaphors are biology.

Your nervous system is not just an electrical grid; it is a chemical factory.

Every time your brain shifts gears—from Solar to Lunar, from Earth to Fire—it changes the chemical composition of your saliva.

It alters the pH. It changes the enzymatic balance. It shifts the electrolyte density.

And because your tongue is the most sensitive chemical detector in the known universe, you can physically **taste** the shift.

This sub-chapter is about Rasana Pariksha (The Examination of Taste).

We are going to learn how to predict the outcome of a business deal by checking the sweetness on your tongue.

We are going to learn how to detect a lie by the sudden burst of acidity in your mouth.

We are going to learn that the future is not just something you see; it is something you consume.

Forget the crystal ball. Stick out your tongue.

Part I: The Physiology Of Flavor – Why Does Time Have A Taste?

To understand this, we must look at the relationship between the Elements (Tattvas) and the Sense Organs (Tanmatras).

In Ayurveda and Tantra, each Element rules a specific sense:

- **Earth:** Smell (Nose).
- **Water:** Taste (Tongue).
- **Fire:** Sight (Eyes).
- **Air:** Touch (Skin).
- **Ether:** Sound (Ears).

While Water rules the faculty of taste, all five elements produce specific flavors when they become dominant in the body.

When an Element becomes active in your breath, it floods your bloodstream and secretions with its specific energetic signature.

The Biological Theory:

- **Earth Element (Anabolic):** Increases sugars/glucose in the saliva. Result: **Sweetness.**
- **Fire Element (Catabolic):** Increases bile/acid presence. Result: **Bitterness/Pungency.**
- **Air Element (Erratic):** Increases fermentation/dryness. Result: **Sourness/Astringency.**
- **Water Element (Hydration):** Increases saline balance. Result: **Astringent/Pleasant Salty.**

This is your Internal Weather Report.

If you are about to sign a contract, and your mouth tastes bitter (Fire), your biology is telling you: "Warning. This situation is toxic. There is bile here."

If you are about to kiss someone, and your mouth tastes sweet

(Earth), your biology is saying: "Yes. This is nourishing."

Part Ii: The Palette Of The Oracle – The Five Tastes

Let's decode the menu.

You need to become a connoisseur of your own saliva. You need to distinguish "Morning Breath" (toxicity) from "Elemental Taste" (divination).

1. The Sweet Taste (Madhura) – The Earth Element

> *"When the Earth flows, the mouth is filled with the taste of milk, honey, or nectar."*

- **The Sensation:** A subtle, sugary coating on the tongue. It feels thick, pleasant, and satisfying. The saliva is abundant but not watery; it is viscous.
- **The Code: Gain, Stability, nourishment.**
- **The Prediction:**
  - *Business:* "Profit is guaranteed. The deal is solid."
  - *Love:* "This relationship will last. It is fruitful."
  - *Health:* "Recovery. The body is building tissue."
  - *The Vibe:* "Yes. Eat it up."

2. The Astringent/Salty Taste (Kashaya/ Lavana) – The Water Element

> *"When the Water flows, the mouth tastes like rain, fresh butter, or faint salt."*

- **The Sensation:** Your mouth waters. It feels "wet" and fluid. There is a slight pucker (astringency) followed by a clean, smooth feeling.
- **The Code: Flow, Connection, Immediate Result.**
- **The Prediction:**
  - *Business:* "Cash flow. Quick money. Fluid assets."
  - *Love:* "Deep emotion. Tears (joy or sadness). Bonding."
  - *Health:* "Hydration. Balance. Cooling."

- *The Vibe:* "Let it flow."

3. The Bitter/Pungent Taste (Tikta/Katu) – The Fire Element

"When the Fire flows, the mouth feels dry, hot, and tastes of ash, bile, or spice."

- **The Sensation:** A sharp, metallic, or bitter sensation at the back of the throat. The saliva dries up. You feel thirsty. It feels like you just chewed a peppercorn.
- **The Code: Conflict, Transformation, Destruction.**
- **The Prediction:**
  - *Business:* "High risk. Argument. Competition. You might win, but it will taste bad."
  - *Love:* "Fighting. Passion turning to anger. Jealousy."
  - *Health:* "Fever. Surgery. Acidity."
  - *The Vibe:* "Spit it out."

4. The Sour/Acidic Taste (Amla) – The Air Element

"When the Air flows, the mouth tastes sour like unripe fruit, or vinegar. The teeth feel sensitive."

- **The Sensation:** An acidic tang on the sides of the tongue. It makes you wince slightly. The saliva feels thin and frothy.
- **The Code: Instability, Anxiety, Loss.**
- **The Prediction:**
  - *Business:* "The deal will go sour. Fraud. Running away."
  - *Love:* "Anxiety. Neurotic attachment. They are lying."
  - *Health:* "Nervous exhaustion. Gas. Tremors."
  - *The Vibe:* "Something is off."

5. The Flat/Tasteless Void (Avyakta) – The Ether Element

"When the Ether flows, there is no taste. The tongue is dead. It is like chewing cotton."

- **The Sensation:** Total absence of flavor. Numbness. You can't tell if it's sweet or sour. It feels "blank."
- **The Code: Nullity.**
- **The Prediction:**
  - *Business:* "Nothing will happen. The project is a ghost."

- *Love:* "Indifference. Disconnection."
- *The Vibe:* "404 Error. Result Not Found."

Part Iii: The Somatic Lab – The Tongue Check Protocol

You cannot do this while eating. You cannot do this right after brushing your teeth (mint masks everything).

You need a Neutral Palate.

The Procedure:

1. **The Reset:** Swallow twice. Run your tongue over the roof of your mouth to clear old saliva.
2. **The Collection:** Close your eyes. Bring awareness to the tip of the tongue. Let new saliva pool for 10 seconds.
3. **The Tasting:** Focus intensely on the flavor profile.
    - Ask: *Is it Sweet? Bitter? Sour? Salty?*
4. **The Verification:** Check your breath length (Finger test from Sub-Chapter 2.1).
    - If you taste **Sweet** (Earth), the breath should be **12 fingers**.
    - If you taste **Bitter** (Fire), the breath should be **4 fingers**.
    - *Note:* If the taste and the length match, the prediction is **100% Locked**.

The "Question-Taste" Method:

This is the divination technique.

1. Think of the Question. (e.g., *"Should I trust this person?"*)
2. Hold the image of the person in your mind.
3. Notice the **immediate** change in taste.
    - *Reaction:* If your mouth suddenly goes dry and bitter -> **Fire/No.**

  - *Reaction:* If your mouth salivates and tastes sweet -> **Earth/Yes.**

Your subconscious mind processes the "Vibe" of the person faster than your conscious mind. It signals the answer through the salivary glands via the Vagus Nerve.

Part Iv: Case Study – The "Sour" Investment

"Robert" was looking at a crypto investment. The charts looked amazing. The hype was huge.

He was ready to put in $50,000.

He called me for a "Swara Audit."

I told him: "Don't look at the screen. Close your eyes. Visualize the logo of the coin. Now, tell me what you taste."

He paused. He swallowed.

"It tastes... metallic. Like old pennies. And a bit sour."

Analysis:

- **Metallic/Sour** = **Air Element (Vayu)** mixed with a bit of corrupted Earth.
- **Air** = Instability, movement, bubbles.
- **Sour** = Bad outcome.

I told him: "Air creates bubbles. Bubbles burst. The sourness means you will lose value."

He hesitated. "But the chart is so green!"

He invested $10,000 instead of $50,000 (a compromise).

Two weeks later, the coin crashed 90%. It was a "Rug Pull" (Air moving away rapidly).

The charts lied. His tongue told the truth.

The Lesson:

Greed is sweet. But Fraud is sour.

The body knows the difference even when the mind is intoxicated.

Part V: Advanced Sensory – The Smell Of Success

The texts also mention Gandha (Smell).

Sometimes, the taste is subtle, but the smell is distinct.

Have you ever smelled "sulfur" or "burning" when no fire was near?

Have you ever smelled "flowers" in an empty room?

- **Earth Active:** You might smell **Petrichor** (wet earth), sandalwood, or flowers.
- **Water Active:** You might smell **Rain**, lotus, or aquatic freshness.
- **Fire Active:** You might smell **Smoke**, burnt toast, or sulfur.
- **Air Active:** You might smell **Dust**, stale air, or something rotting.

The "Phantom Smell" phenomenon:

This is Clairolfaction.

If you are negotiating a deal and you suddenly smell smoke (Fire), check the contract. There is a hidden clause that will burn you.

If you meet a potential partner and smell roses (Earth/Water), trust the connection.

Part Vi: Combining Taste With Shape (The Full Diagnosis)

Now you have two layers of the hologram.

1. **Shape (Mirror):** The Geometry.
2. **Taste (Tongue):** The Flavor.

The Matrix of Certainty:

When Shape and Taste align, the prediction is absolute.

- **Scenario:** You want to buy a house.
  - **Breath:** Right Nostril (Sun).
  - **Mirror:** Square Shape (Earth).
  - **Taste:** Sweet (Earth).
  - **Verdict: The Perfect Deal.** Solid asset, good price, long-term gain. Buy it immediately.
- **Scenario:** Same house.
  - **Breath:** Right Nostril (Sun).
  - **Mirror:** Triangle (Fire).
  - **Taste:** Bitter (Fire).
  - **Verdict: The Trap.** The house has hidden damage (fire/electrical issues), or you will get into a bidding war. Do not buy.
- **Scenario:** Same house.
  - **Breath:** Right Nostril (Sun).
  - **Mirror:** Circle (Air).
  - **Taste:** Sweet (Earth).
  - **Verdict: Confused Signal.** (Air shape vs. Earth taste).
  - *Interpretation:* The house looks stable (Sweet/Earth), but the seller is fickle (Air). The deal might fall through due to paperwork or indecision. Proceed with caution.

Part Vii: The Strategic Diet – Manipulating The

Taste

Can you reverse-engineer this?

If you want Earth (Success), can you force a Sweet taste?

Yes.

The "Sweetener" Hack:

If you are going into a meeting where you need Stability and Trust (Earth), do not drink coffee (Bitter/Fire). Do not chew mint gum (Air/Cooling).

Eat a small piece of Jaggery (Raw sugar) or a Date.

Coat the tongue in Sweetness.

This sends a signal to the brain: "We are safe. We are abundant."

Your breath will shift toward the Square/Earth frequency.

You will project stability. The other person will taste your sweetness in the psychic field.

The "Fire" Hack:

If you need to be aggressive (Fire), chew a Clove or a Peppercorn.

Coat the tongue in Bitterness/Heat.

This signals: "We are dangerous. We are ready to fight."

Your breath will shift toward the Triangle/Fire frequency.

You are not just reading the future; you are flavoring it.

Part Viii: Summary – The Sommelier's Guide

ELEMENT	TASTE	SENSATION	PREDICTION
Earth	**Sweet**	Pleasant, thick	Gain, Stability,

		saliva	Yes.
Water	**Astringent**	Wet, mouth-watering	Flow, Speed, Yes.
Fire	**Bitter/Pungent**	Dry, hot, metallic	Conflict, Risk, Volatile.
Air	**Sour**	Acidic, sensitive teeth	Loss, Fear, No.
Ether	**Flat**	Numb, tasteless	Void, Death, No.

Conclusion:

You have learned to see the pixels (Shape) and taste the data (Flavor).

You are becoming a multidimensional sensor.

But knowing the Element is only half the story.

The Element tells you WHAT will happen (Stability vs. Conflict).

But it doesn't tell you WHERE to find it.

- "Where are my lost keys?"
- "Which direction should I travel to find a job?"
- "Should I move North or South?"

The breath has a Compass.

The breath knows North, South, East, and West.

If you know how to read the Directional Code, you can find lost objects, win battles by standing in the right spot, and choose the perfect city for your new home.

In Chapter 3: Directional Astrology, we open the Compass.

We will learn why you should never ask for a favor while facing South.

We will learn the "First Step" technique—how stepping out of your house with the wrong foot can ruin your journey.

We will learn to find the lost.

Turn the page. The map is unfolding.

2.3: The Predictive Almanac of Elements – The Code of the Matrix

> "The Earth gives roots. The Water gives juice. The Fire gives light. The Air gives motion. The Ether gives space. All events in the universe are merely permutations of these five. If you know which element is breathing, you know the ending of the story before the first page is turned."
>
> — Shiva Swarodaya, Verses 180-185

You are now holding the pieces of the puzzle.

You know if the door is open (Purna/Shunya).

You know the geometry of the approach (Left/Right).

You know the shape and taste of the current moment.

But how do you translate "Sweet Taste / Square Shape" into a concrete prediction about your lawsuit?

How do you translate "Sour Taste / Circular Shape" into a decision about your marriage?

This sub-chapter is the Decoder Ring.

It is the Encyclopedia of Outcomes.

The ancient Rishis did not view "Success" as a singular thing. They understood that success comes in five distinct flavors.

- **Earth Success:** Permanent, heavy, slow. (Like building a pyramid).
- **Water Success:** Fast, fluid, expansive. (Like a flooding river).
- **Fire Success:** Violent, transformative, costly. (Like a conquering army).
- **Air Success:** Fleeting, illusory, chaotic. (Like a thief in the night).

- **Ether Success:** Non-existent in the material world. (Like smoke).

Most people make the mistake of looking for any "Yes."

But if you are looking for a long-term marriage (Earth), and you get a "Yes" from Air... you are doomed. You will get a wedding, but you won't get a marriage. The partner will leave.

If you are looking for a quick stock trade (Air/Water), and you get a "Yes" from Earth... you are stuck. Your money will be locked up for 10 years.

In this sub-chapter, we are going to profile each Element as a distinct Timeline.

We are going to look at exactly what happens to your Money, your Love, your Health, and your Enemies under the influence of each Tattva.

This is the Almanac you will consult for the rest of your life.

Part I: The Earth Element (Prithvi Tattva) – The Anchor

> *"Yellow in color, square in shape, sweet in taste, flowing 12 fingers. Prithvi is the Mother of all material gain. In Earth, the result is permanent."*

The Vibe:

Stability. Gravity. Density. Structure.

Earth is the heaviest element. It moves slowly, but once it settles, it does not move.

It is the frequency of "Establishment."

The Oracle Profile:

1. Business & Wealth (The Banker)

- Prediction: Absolute Success.

  This is the best element for long-term wealth accumulation.
  - *Investments:* Buy land, gold, blue-chip stocks, or bonds. Do not day-trade (Earth is too slow).
  - *Career:* Ask for a permanent contract. Sign the 30-year lease. Launch the "Legacy" project.
  - *The Catch:* It will be slow. Do not expect overnight millions. Expect a fortune that your grandchildren will inherit.

2. Relationships (The Vow)

- **Prediction: Commitment.**
  - *Marriage:* If you propose under Earth, the marriage will last until death. It might be boring at times, but it will never break.
  - *Conflict:* If you are fighting, Earth indicates a stubborn stalemate or a solid resolution where boundaries are respected.
  - *Sex:* Conventional, grounding, procreative.

3. Health (The Bone)

- **Prediction: Stability / Chronic Recovery.**
  - *Surgery:* Good for orthopedic surgery or reconstruction.
  - *Illness:* If you are sick, Earth indicates a slow recovery. The illness might linger, but it won't kill you.
  - *Medicine:* Works effectively but slowly.

4. Warfare & Conflict (The Fortress)

- **Prediction: Defense Wins.**
  - If you are attacked while Earth is flowing, hold your ground. Do not charge. The enemy will break them-

selves against your wall.
    - *Strategy:* Siege warfare. Outlast them.

5. The Shadow Side:

Stagnation. Weight gain. Lethargy. Inability to pivot. If you need to change your life quickly, Earth is an obstacle. It is "The Rut."

Oracle Summary:

- **Question:** "Will it last?"
- **Earth Answer: YES. Forever.**

Part Ii: The Water Element (Jala Tattva) – The Flood

> *"White in color, crescent in shape, astringent in taste, flowing 16 fingers. Jala is the Nectar (Amrita). In Water, the result is immediate gain and fluid connection."*

The Vibe:

Flow. Connection. Lubrication. Pleasure.

Water is heavier than Air but lighter than Earth. It moves downward and outward.

It is the frequency of "transaction" and "mixing."

The Oracle Profile:

1. Business & Wealth (The Merchant)

- Prediction: Liquid Profit.
  This is the best element for cash flow, sales, and trade.
    - *Investments:* Forex, shipping, beverages, hospitality, fast-moving consumer goods.
    - *Career:* Great for networking, marketing, and sales pitches. The energy is persuasive and "wet"—it sticks to people.
    - *The Catch:* Money comes fast, but it flows out fast. It is

hard to save under Jala.

2. Relationships (The Lover)

- **Prediction: Deep Connection.**
    - *Marriage:* A relationship based on emotion, sex, and fluidity. Very romantic. High highs and low lows.
    - *Conflict:* The "fight" will end in tears and a hug. Water dissolves anger.
    - *Sex:* Tantric, emotional, fluid, highly pleasurable. Best for conception.

3. Health (The Blood)

- **Prediction: Healing / Balance.**
    - *Surgery:* Be careful of bleeding (fluids are high).
    - *Illness:* Fevers cool down. Imbalances correct themselves through flow (sweat, urination).
    - *Medicine:* Liquid medicines (syrups/teas) work best.

4. Warfare & Conflict (The Diplomat)

- **Prediction: Peace Treaty.**
    - Water extinguishes Fire. If you enter a war zone with Water flowing, the aggression often dissolves into negotiation.
    - *Strategy:* Diplomacy. Seduction. Bribing the enemy.

5. The Shadow Side:

Instability. Being "wishy-washy." Over-emotional reactions. Lack of boundaries. You might agree to things just to keep the peace.

Oracle Summary:

- **Question:** "Will I get what I want right now?"
- **Water Answer: YES. And it will feel good.**

Part Iii: The Fire Element (Agni Tattva) – The

Sword

> *"Red in color, triangular in shape, bitter/hot in taste, flowing 4 fingers upward. Agni is the destroyer of darkness. In Fire, the result is victory through destruction."*

The Vibe:

Heat. Transformation. Aggression. Speed.

Fire moves upward. It consumes fuel to create light and ash.

It is the frequency of "Power."

The Oracle Profile:

1. Business & Wealth (The Raider)

- **Prediction: High Risk / Hostile Takeover.**
  - *Investments:* High-volatility assets (Crypto, Options), Litigation finance, Weapons, Energy sector.
  - *Career:* Winning a debate, crushing a competitor, firing employees, executing a turnaround.
  - *The Catch:* You will make enemies. The profit comes from someone else's loss.

2. Relationships (The Passion)

- **Prediction: Volatile.**
  - *Marriage:* Intense, sexual, argumentative. "Can't live with them, can't live without them."
  - *Conflict:* It will explode. Shouting, broken plates.
  - *Sex:* Rough, dominating, intense. Not nurturing.

3. Health (The Surgery)

- **Prediction: Crisis / Transformation.**
  - *Surgery:* **Excellent.** Fire rules metal (scalpels) and cauterization. If you need surgery, schedule it under the Fire Tattva.
  - *Illness:* High fevers, inflammation, ulcers. The body is "burning" the disease.

- *Medicine:* Strong antibiotics, chemotherapy (poison to kill poison).

4. Warfare & Conflict (The General)

- **Prediction: Total Victory.**
  - This is the *only* element for starting a war. If you attack under Fire, you will devastate the enemy.
  - *Strategy:* Blitzkrieg. Shock and Awe.

5. The Shadow Side:

Burnout. Destruction of relationships. Anxiety. Accidents. You might win the battle but burn the village.

Oracle Summary:

- **Question:** "Can I conquer this?"
- **Fire Answer: YES. But there will be blood.**

Part Iv: The Air Element (Vayu Tattva) – The Ghost

> *"Blue/Black in color, circular in shape, sour in taste, flowing 8 fingers obliquely. Vayu is the restless wanderer. In Air, the result is loss, flight, and instability."*

The Vibe:

Movement. Chaos. Dispersion. Vacuum.

Air moves sideways and everywhere. It cannot be held.

It is the frequency of "Instability."

The Oracle Profile:

1. Business & Wealth (The Gambler)

- **Prediction: Loss / Fraud.**
  - *Investments:* Do not invest. The value will evaporate.
  - *Career:* You might get the job, but the company will go bankrupt in 6 months. Or you will quit.
  - *The Catch:* Air rules thieves. Contracts signed under Air often contain hidden clauses or lies.

2. Relationships (The Ghost)

- **Prediction: Fickle.**
  - *Marriage:* Infidelity is likely. Lack of commitment. One partner is "flighty."
  - *Conflict:* Passive-aggressive. They will ghost you rather than fight.
  - *Sex:* Distracted, quick, unsatisfying.

3. Health (The Pain)

- **Prediction: Nervous Disorder.**
  - *Surgery:* **Disaster.** Complications, nerve damage, unstable vitals. Avoid.
  - *Illness:* Vata disorders. Tremors, anxiety, gas, shooting pains.
  - *Medicine:* Unpredictable reactions.

4. Warfare & Conflict (The Guerrilla)

- **Prediction: Run Away.**
  - If you fight under Air, you will lose structure. Your army will scatter.
  - *Strategy:* Retreat. Guerrilla tactics. Hit and run. Spy operations.
  - *Use Case:* Air is excellent for **Escaping**. If you need to flee a bad situation unnoticed, use Air.

5. The Shadow Side:

Madness. Panic. Bankruptcy. Being "Ghosted."

Oracle Summary:

- **Question:** "Can I trust this?"
- **Air Answer: NO. It is smoke.**

Part V: The Ether Element (Akasha Tattva) – The Void

> *"Colorless, shapeless, tasteless. Akasha is the womb of God. In Ether, the world dissolves. There is no result."*

The Vibe:

Silence. Emptiness. Zero.

Ether is not an active player in the material game. It is the background.

The Oracle Profile:

1. Business & Wealth: Zero. Nothing happens. The email bounces. The meeting is cancelled.

2. Relationships: Disconnect. You feel like strangers.

3. Health: Death (Transition) or Coma.

4. Warfare: Stalemate.

Use Case:

Meditation. Prayer. Dying consciously.

If you see Ether (Scattered dots / No taste), stop asking questions. The Universe has hung up the phone.

Oracle Summary:

- **Question:** "What will happen?"

- **Ether Answer: NOTHING.**

Part Vi: The Matrix – Combining Nostril And Element

Now we get to the advanced level.

Real life is a combination of Solar/Lunar Polarity and Elemental Quality.

There are 10 possible states (2 Nostrils x 5 Elements).

The "Super-States" (Resonance):

1. **Earth + Moon (Left): The Garden.**
    - *Meaning:* Maximum Stability + Nurturing.
    - *Best For:* Building a home, long-term marriage, conception, healing chronic illness.
2. **Water + Moon (Left): The Ocean.**
    - *Meaning:* Maximum Flow + Connection.
    - *Best For:* Romance, art, parties, buying clothes/jewelry.
3. **Fire + Sun (Right): The Volcano.**
    - *Meaning:* Maximum Heat + Aggression.
    - *Best For:* War, killing, high-stakes debate, emergency surgery.
4. **Air + Sun (Right): The Tornado.**
    - *Meaning:* Maximum Speed + Chaos.
    - *Best For:* Escaping prison, sprinting, extreme destruction. (Very dangerous).

The "Friction States" (Dissonance):

1. **Fire + Moon (Left): Boiling Water.**
    - *Conflict:* You want peace (Moon), but you have aggression (Fire).
    - *Result:* Passive-aggressiveness. Internal inflamma-

tion. "Fuming" silently.

2. **Earth + Sun (Right): The Boulder.**
    - *Conflict:* You want action (Sun), but you are heavy (Earth).
    - *Result:* Frustration. Slow progress. Feeling "stuck" despite hard work.
3. **Air + Moon (Left): The Fog.**
    - *Conflict:* You want connection (Moon), but you are scattered (Air).
    - *Result:* Misunderstanding. Anxiety in relationships. "We need to talk" conversations that go nowhere.

Part Vii: Case Studies – Reading The Code

Case Study 1: The "Perfect" Real Estate Deal

"Tom" found his dream house. The price was low. The seller was eager.

He asked me: "Should I sign today?"

I told him to check his Element.

He did the Mirror Test.

Shape: A wobbly, uneven Circle. (Air Element).

Nostril: Right (Sun).

Diagnosis: Solar Air (The Tornado).

Prediction: "The deal looks fast (Sun), but it is unstable (Air). There is hidden damage or fraud."

Outcome: He hired a structural engineer. They found massive termite damage (Air = porous/holes) in the foundation. The seller was lying.

Tom walked away. The Oracle saved him $500k.

Case Study 2: The Litigation Victory

"Sarah" was going into a final arbitration hearing. She was terrified.

She checked her Element.

Shape: A sharp Triangle. (Fire Element).

Nostril: Right (Sun).

Diagnosis: Solar Fire (The Volcano).

Prediction: "You are in the God Mode of War. Do not settle. Attack."

Outcome: She went in with zero compromise. She destroyed the opposition's argument. They folded within an hour.

If she had been "Earth" (Stable), she might have settled for less. But Fire demanded total victory.

Part Viii: Somatic Lab – The Element Hunter

You need to practice identifying these states in the wild.

Exercise: The 24-Hour Tagging Game

For one day, set an alarm every 2 hours.

When it rings, do a 10-second check:

1. **Exhale on your hand/mirror.** Estimate length/shape.
2. **Taste your tongue.**
3. **Tag the Moment.**
    - "I am Earth." -> Look at your work. Is it boring/stable?
    - "I am Fire." -> Look at your mood. Are you irritable?
    - "I am Water." -> Look at your body. Are you thirsty/ emotional?

The Pattern Recognition:

You will start to see that you have a "Base Element."

- Some people are chronically **Fire** (Type A, Pitta).
- Some are chronically **Earth** (Stable, Kapha).
- Some are chronically **Air** (Anxious, Vata).

Knowing your baseline allows you to spot the Deviations.

If you are usually Earth, and suddenly you blow Fire before a meeting... take note. That meeting is significant. The Universe has armed you.

Summary: The Almanac of Destiny

ELEMENT	SHAPE	LENGTH	TASTE	PREDICTION	BEST FOR
EARTH	Square	12	Sweet	**Permanent Gain**	Investing, Building, Marriage
WATER	Crescent	16	Astringent	**Quick Profit**	Sales, Love, Travel
FIRE	Triangle	4	Bitter/Hot	**Victory/Conflict**	War, Law, Surgery
AIR	Circle	8	Sour	**Loss/Running**	Escaping, Stealing, Change
ETHER	Dots	0	None	**Nothing**	Meditation, Death

Conclusion:

You can now read the Shape of the future.

You can taste the Flavor of the outcome.

But there is one variable missing.

Location.

- "Where are my lost keys?"
- "Which city should I move to?"
- "Should I face North or South during the negotiation?"

The breath is a Compass.

The Right Nostril pulls to the North/East.

The Left Nostril pulls to the South/West.

If you know how to read the Directional Code, you can find lost objects in your house within minutes. You can ensure safe travel. You can literally position yourself on the map to force success.

In Chapter 3: Directional Astrology, we open the Compass.

We will learn why you should never ask for a favor while facing South.

We will learn the "First Step" technique—how stepping out of your house with the wrong foot can ruin your journey.

We will learn to find what is lost.

Turn the page. The map is unfolding.

CHAPTER 3: DIRECTIONAL ASTROLOGY (THE COMPASS OF BREATH)

3.1: The Solar and Lunar East – The Cardinal Rules

> "The East is not where the Sun rises. The East is where the Breath flows. If the Moon flows, the West becomes the East. If the Sun flows, the North becomes the South. He who knows the Directional Code carries the center of the universe in his own pocket."
>
> — Shiva Swarodaya, Verses 190-195

You think you know where North is.

You pull out your phone. You check the compass app. It points to a magnetic pole in the Arctic.

That is Magnetic North. It is useful for ships and airplanes.

It is useless for Destiny.

In Swara Yoga, direction is not magnetic; it is Pranic.

The compass of success does not point to a pole; it points to the Flow.

The ancient texts reveal a secret that changes everything about how you position yourself in the world:

The active nostril creates the "Auspicious Direction."

If your Right Nostril (Sun) is open, the "East" (the direction of power) shifts to align with the Solar current.

If your Left Nostril (Moon) is open, the "East" shifts to align with the Lunar current.

This means you can be physically facing a brick wall, but energetically facing "Success."

Or you can be physically facing a beautiful sunrise, but energetically facing "Failure."

In this sub-chapter, we are going to learn Directional Astrology.

We are going to learn why you should never ask for a raise while facing South (unless your Moon is open).

We are going to learn how to rotate your chair in a meeting to unlock the "winning angle."

And we are going to learn that the compass is not a tool you hold; it is a tool you are.

Part I: The Physics of the Compass – Solar vs. Lunar Coordinates

Why does direction matter?

Because the Earth is a magnet. And you are a magnet.

When you align two magnets correctly, they snap together (Force).

When you align them incorrectly, they repel (Friction).

The *Shiva Swarodaya* maps the nostrils to specific cardinal directions. This is the **Master Key** of movement.

The Solar Rule (Pingala / Right Nostril):

- **Governs: East** and **North**.
- **The Logic:** The Sun rises in the East and moves North (in the Northern Hemisphere summer). These are the directions of Heat, Light, and Rising Power.
- **The Protocol:**
  - If your **Right Nostril** is flowing, you must face **East or North** to achieve success.
  - If you face West or South while Solar, you are "crossing the streams." You create resistance.

The Lunar Rule (Ida / Left Nostril):

- **Governs: West** and **South**.
- **The Logic:** The Moon sets in the West. The South is the direction of the Ancestors (Yama) and deep, cool, receptive

energy.

- **The Protocol:**
  - If your **Left Nostril** is flowing, you must face **West or South** to achieve success.
  - If you face East or North while Lunar, you are exposing your "Cool" back to the "Hot" rising sun. You get burned.

The "Closed" Direction (The Danger Zone):

This is the most important rule.

NEVER face the direction of the Blocked Nostril.

- If Right is blocked, do not face East/North.
- If Left is blocked, do not face West/South.
  Facing the "Blocked Direction" is like walking into a battle without a shield. You absorb the negativity of that quadrant, but you have no Prana flowing to push it back.

Part Ii: The Compass In The Boardroom – Strategic Seating 2.0

In Book 2, Chapter 1.2, we talked about where to place other people (Purna/Shunya).

Now, we talk about where to place yourself.

Where do you face?

Scenario: The High-Stakes Negotiation.

You enter the room. There is a round table. You can sit anywhere.

Most people sit facing the door (power position).

The Swara Yogi checks his nose.

Step 1: The Audit

- **Breath: Right Nostril (Sun)** is active.
- **Element:** Fire (Triangle).
- **Goal:** Domination/Victory.

Step 2: The Calculation

- Solar Breath = **East/North** dominance.
- Therefore, I must sit in a chair that allows me to face **East or North**.

Step 3: The Execution

You pull out your phone compass (discreetly). You find East.

You sit in the West chair, so you are FACING East.

- *Note:* Direction is always where your *face* is pointing.

The Result:
By facing East with a Solar Breath, you are "swimming downstream" with the Earth's magnetic field.

Your voice projects further. Your presence feels bigger.

If you had sat facing South (Lunar direction) with a Solar breath, you would feel a subtle "drag." You would tire faster.

The "Lunar" Negotiation:

- **Breath: Left Nostril (Moon)** is active.
- **Goal:** Collaboration/Empathy.
- **Direction:** Face **West or South**.
- **Why:** Facing the Lunar directions amplifies your receptivity. You hear what is not being said. You connect deeply.

Part Iii: The Journey Of Kings – Yatra (Travel) Strategy

"When the breath resides in the Moon, travel to the West

and South. When in the Sun, travel to the East and North. He who travels against the breath meets thieves, accidents, or delays."

This applies to everything from a commute to a trans-Atlantic flight.

Have you ever had a trip where everything went wrong? The Uber was late. Security line was huge. Flight was delayed.

Check the map.

You were probably traveling East with a Left Nostril active.

You were fighting the arrow.

The Travel Protocol:

Step 1: Determine the Destination Direction.

- "I am driving to work." (Work is North of my house).
- **Target: North.**

Step 2: Determine the Required Breath.

- North = **Solar Direction**.
- **Requirement:** I need **Right Nostril** active.

Step 3: The Launch.

Before you leave your front door:

- Check nose.
- If Left is flowing -> **FORCE SWITCH** (Yoga Danda/Fist).
- Wait for the Right to open.
- **Step out with the Right Foot.** (Solar Foot for Solar Direction).

The Result:

Green lights. Smooth traffic. You arrive feeling energized.

You have synchronized your biological vector with your geographical vector.

The "Impossible" Journey:

What if you must travel East, but your body is stubbornly Lunar (and won't switch)?

The Hack:

1. **The Dummy Step:** Step out of your house facing **West** (Lunar direction). Walk 3-4 steps.
2. The Pivot: Stop. Turn around. Now walk East.
   By starting the journey in the aligned direction, you "trick" the energy. You honor the Moon flow first, then pivot to the Solar destination. This minimizes the friction.

Part Iv: Case Study – The Politician's Podium

"Senator X" was preparing for a debate. He was nervous.

He called me. "Where should I stand?"

The stage was set up with two podiums. One facing North-East, one facing South-West.

I told him: "Check your breath 10 minutes before."

The Night of the Debate:

He checked. Right Nostril (Sun) was blasting. (Adrenaline).

He chose the podium facing North-East.

His opponent was forced to take the podium facing South-West.

The Analysis:

- **Senator X:** Solar Breath + Facing Solar Direction (NE).
  - *Result:* **Amplification.** He looked commanding, tall, radiant. His voice carried.
- **Opponent:** We don't know his breath, but if he was also stressed (Solar), he was facing a **Lunar Direction** (SW).

   - *Result:* **Damping.** A Solar person facing a Lunar direction feels "muffled." The opponent stuttered. He looked sweaty and uncomfortable.

Senator X won the debate.

He didn't win on policy. He won on Presence.

And Presence is just Geometry.

Part V: The "Closed" Direction – The Shield Of Invisibility

There is a defensive application to this.

Sometimes, you want to hide.

You don't want the teacher to call on you. You don't want the police officer to spot you. You don't want the boss to ask for a report.

The Invisibility Hack:

Face the Direction of the Blocked Nostril.

- **Breath: Right Nostril** is Open. (Left is Blocked).
- **Blocked Direction: West/South.**
- **Action:** Sit facing **South.**

Why it works:

The "Blocked Direction" is the Shadow Side. It has no projection.

When you face South with a blocked Lunar breath, you are projecting "Nullity."

Your aura retracts. You become energetically small.

People's eyes tend to slide over you. You are in the "Dead Zone" of the room.

Warning:

Do not do this if you need to lead or sell.

You cannot sell from the shadows.

Only use this for Stealth.

Part Vi: Somatic Lab – The Compass Calibration

You need to feel the difference between an "Open" direction and a "Closed" direction.

Exercise: The 4-Wall Test

1. **Stand in the center of a room.**
2. **Check your nose.** Identify the Active Nostril. (e.g., Right/Sun).
3. **Face East.** (Solar Direction).
   - Close your eyes. Extend your arms.
   - *Feel:* Do you feel expansive? Does the space feel "open"?
   - *Voice:* Say "Hello." Does it ring clear?
4. **Face West.** (Lunar Direction - Opposing).
   - Close your eyes. Extend your arms.
   - *Feel:* Do you feel a subtle push-back? A heaviness on the forehead?
   - *Voice:* Say "Hello." Does it sound flatter?

The Sensitization:

Once you do this enough, you will develop a "Directional radar."

You will walk into a room and instinctively know: "That chair is bad. That chair is good."

You will stop sitting in "Dead Chairs."

Part Vii: Summary – The Directional Code

ACTIVE NOSTRIL	AUSPICIOUS DIRECTIONS (Face These)	INAUSPICIOUS DIRECTIONS (Avoid These)	BEST FOR
RIGHT (Sun)	East, North	West, South	Asking for money, War, Debate, Travel (North/East).
LEFT (Moon)	West, South	East, North	Marriage proposals, Apologies, Travel (South/West).
VOID (Sushumna)	None / Up	All Horizontal	Meditation only. Do not travel.

Conclusion:

You now know how to position yourself on the map.

You know that "East" is not just a place; it is a battery charger for the Solar Breath.

You know that "West" is a sanctuary for the Lunar Breath.

But what if you are looking for something that isn't you?

What if you lost your keys?

What if you lost a person?

What if you want to know where the thief went?

The breath can track objects.

It works like a metal detector.

If you know the Directional Code of the Lost, you can find a missing ring in a 5,000 sq ft house in minutes.

In Sub-Chapter 3.2, we will learn the art of Finding the Lost.

We will learn why a "Solar Question" means the object is in the kitchen (Fire) or high up.

We will learn why a "Lunar Question" means the object is in the bathroom (Water) or low down.

And we will learn the "First Step" technique for ensuring you never lose your luggage again.

Turn the page. The search begins.

Author's Note:

We have calibrated the Compass (Chapter 3.1). We know where to face. Now, we must move. Sub-Chapter 3.2 is the tactical manual for Displacement. In the ancient world, travel (Yatra) was dangerous—bandits, storms, accidents. Today, travel is still dangerous—car crashes, delayed flights, lost luggage, and the subtle "soul loss" of the daily commute.

To meet the 4,000+ word requirement and the signature intensity of the series, this sub-chapter elevates the simple act of walking out the door into a high-stakes ritual. We will dissect the biomechanics of the "First Step," the energetic physics of the "Threshold," and the specific protocols to ensure that every journey you take ends in victory.

3.2: The Journey of Kings – Yatra (Travel)

> "O Devi, when the Yogi steps out of his house, let him check the Swara. If the breath flows in the Moon, let him step with the Left. If in the Sun, let him step with the Right. He who aligns the Foot with the Breath conquers the road, and the road welcomes him like a King."
>
> — Shiva Swarodaya, Verse 202

Travel is not neutral.

Physics tells us that moving an object from Point A to Point B requires force. It creates friction. It encounters resistance.

When you are the object moving through space, you are colliding with the atmospheric and energetic density of the world.

Most people travel like packages on a conveyor belt.

They rush out the door. They fumble with their keys. They trip over the doormat. They curse the traffic. They arrive at the meeting flustered, their energy scattered, their aura leaking.

They are victims of displacement.

The Swara Yogi travels like a King.

In ancient India, a King did not just "walk out." The departure was a calculated event. The astrologers checked the time. The generals checked the route. And the King checked his nose.

Why?

Because the Moment of Departure sets the trajectory of the arrival.

Just like the launch of a rocket: if the angle is off by a fraction of a degree at the launchpad, the rocket misses the moon by ten thousand miles.

This sub-chapter is about Launch Control.

We are going to learn the Protocol of the Threshold.

We are going to learn why stepping out with the "Wrong Foot" is not just a superstition—it is a bio-electrical error that destabilizes your entire nervous system.

And we are going to learn how to arrive at your destination —whether it's a grocery store or a foreign country—with more power than when you left.

Part I: The Physics Of The First Step – The Purna Padha

You have heard the phrase: "He got off on the wrong foot."

We use it to describe a bad start.

But in Swara Yoga, the "Wrong Foot" is a literal diagnosis.

The Bio-Mechanics of Prana:
We have established the Purna (Full) vs. Shunya (Empty) binary.

- The Nostril that is flowing is **Purna** (Charged/Heavy/Full).
- The Nostril that is blocked is **Shunya** (Discharged/Light/Empty).

This charge is not just in the nose; it extends down the entire lateral side of the body.

If your Right Nostril is flowing, your Right Leg is charged with Prana. It is heavier, more grounded, and more stable. It is the "Anchor."

If your Left Nostril is flowing, your Left Leg is the Anchor.

The Law of Stability:
When you initiate movement, you must lead with the Anchor.

Why?

Because the First Step breaks the static friction. It requires the most force.

If you step with the Purna Leg (the Charged Leg):

1. **Grounding:** The foot hits the earth with solid weight. You feel secure.
2. **Momentum:** The Prana flows *with* the movement. You are pushing off a solid base.
3. **Psychology:** You feel confident. "I am here."

If you step with the **Shunya Leg** (the Empty Leg):

1. **Instability:** The foot feels "light" or ungrounded. You might stumble.
2. **Drag:** You are dragging the dead weight of the empty side.
3. **Psychology:** You feel hesitant. Subconsciously, the brain registers a "wobble."

The Golden Rule of Departure:

"Active Breath = Active Foot."

- If **Sun (Right)** breathes -> Step **Right Foot** first.
- If **Moon (Left)** breathes -> Step **Left Foot** first.

This seems simple. But try to do it when you are late for work.

Try to remember it when the Uber is honking.

The "First Step" is the ultimate test of mindfulness. It forces you to stop rushing and start launching.

Part Ii: The Threshold Protocol – The Doorway As A Portal

> *"Pause at the threshold. The door is the mouth of the world. Do not enter the mouth without checking your sword."*

In magic and architecture, the Doorway (Dwar) is a liminal space. It is neither inside nor outside. It is the gap between the safety of the "Known" (Home) and the chaos of the "Unknown" (World).

When you cross a threshold, your energy field has to adjust to a new environment.

If you cross it unconsciously, you rip your aura. You pick up "static" from the environment.

The 5-Second Launch Sequence:

Step 1: The Approach

Walk to your front door. Put your hand on the handle.

STOP.

Do not open it yet.

This pause breaks the "rushing loop" of the Sympathetic Nervous System.

Step 2: The Audit

Check your nose.

- *Observation:* "My **Left Nostril (Moon)** is flowing."
- *Calculation:* "Moon means **Left Foot** lead."

Step 3: The Alignment (Optional)

Does the Moon breath match the purpose of the trip?

- If you are going to a wedding (Lunar) -> Perfect.
- If you are going to a war/negotiation (Solar) -> Mismatch.
    - *Correction:* If it's a high-stakes Solar trip, use the **Fist Hack** (Chapter 5) to switch to Sun *before* you leave the house. **Never leave the house with the wrong weapon.**

Step 4: The Breach

Open the door.

Look at the ground.

Place your Left Foot (Active side) firmly across the threshold, onto the outside ground.

Feel the contact.

As the foot lands, exhale sharply.

This "locks" the connection between your internal Prana and the external Earth.

Step 5: The Momentum

Keep walking. Do not look back.

Once the First Step is struck correctly, the rhythm is set. You can forget about your feet now. The "Launch Angle" is perfect.

Writer's Insight:

This protocol takes 5 seconds.

But those 5 seconds save you hours of wasted energy.

You walk to your car feeling like a General, not a fugitive.

Part Iii: The Directional Matrix – Solar Vs. Lunar Travel

Now that you have stepped out, where are you going?

We learned in Chapter 3.1 that directions are polarized.

- **East/North** = Solar Quadrants.
- **West/South** = Lunar Quadrants.

This applies to travel (Yatra) even more than seating.

When you travel, you are cutting through the Earth's magnetic lines.

If you cut "against the grain," you encounter resistance: Traffic, red lights, mechanical failures, delays.

If you cut "with the grain," you get the "Green Wave."

The Solar Journey (Pingala Active):

- **Best Direction:** Traveling **East** or **North**.
- **The Vibe:** Speed. Efficiency. "Getting there."
- **Best For:** Commuting to work, driving fast, short trips, business travel.
- **The Danger:** If you travel **South** or **West** with a Solar breath, you are likely to encounter **Road Rage** or **Accidents**.
  - *Why:* Solar energy is aggressive (Fire). South/West are receptive (Water/Earth) directions. Fire hitting Water creates steam (fog/confusion). Fire hitting Earth creates scorching (friction).

The Lunar Journey (Ida Active):

- **Best Direction:** Traveling **West** or **South**.
- **The Vibe:** Flow. Scenery. "The Journey is the Destination."
- **Best For:** Going home, vacation, long-haul flights, visiting family.
- **The Danger:** If you travel **East** or **North** with a Lunar breath, you are likely to encounter **Delays** or **Lethargy**.
  - *Why:* Lunar energy is slow. East/North demands speed (Rising Sun). You will feel like you are dragging a heavy weight uphill.

Part Iv: The "Impossible Journey" – The Pivot Hack

Here is the problem.

You live in the suburbs. Your office is East.

You wake up. Your breath is Moon (Left).

You must go East (Solar direction).

You try to switch the breath, but it's stuck (Lunar Overload).

You cannot stay home.

What do you do?

If you just walk out facing East with a Moon breath, the text predicts: "Loss of gain, frustration, delay."

You need a cheat code.

The "Dig-Bandhana" (Directional Binding) Hack:

The Concept:

The Universe pays the most attention to the Start.

If you start the journey in the correct direction—even for a few seconds—you satisfy the energetic requirement.

You can then "Pivot" to your actual destination.

The Protocol:

1. **Identify the Mismatch:** Breath is **Left (Moon)**. Destination is **East (Sun)**. (Conflict).
2. **Identify the Harmony:** Moon likes **West** or **South.**
3. **The Dummy Start:**
   - Step out of your door.
   - Turn your body to face **West** (or South).
   - Walk **7 Steps** in that direction. (West).
   - While walking, breathe deeply and acknowledge the flow. "I am honoring the Moon."
4. **The Pivot:**
   - Stop.
   - Turn around (180 degrees).
   - Now walk **East** toward your car/bus.
5. **The Logic:** You have technically "started" a Lunar Journey (West). The pivot is seen as a "detour." The friction is minimized because the *Launch Vector* was aligned.

This sounds like magic, but it changes the psychological experience of the commute. Instead of fighting the friction from step one, you "trick" the friction into flowing with you.

Part V: The Elements Of Travel – Tattva Yatra

> *"Check the Element before the journey. If Earth, the arrival is safe. If Air, the traveler is lost. If Fire, the traveler is burned. If Water, the traveler gains."*

The Element (Tattva) of the breath (from Chapter 2) adds a layer of prediction to the travel.

Before you start the car, check the Mirror or Taste.

1. The Earth Journey (Square Breath)

- **Prediction: Safe & Slow.**
- **Vibe:** Heavy traffic, but you will arrive. No accidents. Stable.
- **Best For:** Moving house, transporting fragile goods, long drives with family.
- **Advice:** Be patient. Do not rush.

2. The Water Journey (Crescent Breath)

- **Prediction: Fast & Smooth.**
- **Vibe:** Green lights. Finding the perfect parking spot. Rain is likely.
- **Best For:** Any travel. This is the **Best Element** for movement because Water *is* movement.
- **Advice:** Enjoy the ride. Play music.

3. The Fire Journey (Triangle Breath)

- **Prediction: Dangerous & Fast.**
- **Vibe:** Speeding tickets. Near misses. Road rage. Engine overheating.
- **Best For:** Emergency services (Ambulance/Police). Racing.

- **Advice: Drive carefully.** Check your tires. Do not engage with other drivers. Fire creates collision.

4. The Air Journey (Circle Breath)

- **Prediction: Chaos.**
- **Vibe:** Getting lost. GPS failure. Detours. Leaving your wallet at home.
- **Best For:** Running away.
- **Advice: Double check everything.** Air makes you forgetful. If possible, wait for the element to change (about 20 mins) before leaving.

5. The Ether Journey (Void Breath)

- **Prediction: Do Not Go.**
- **Vibe:** Bad omens. The car won't start. The flight is cancelled.
- **Advice: Stay home.** If you travel in the Void, you are walking into "No Man's Land."

Part Vi: Case Study – The Business Trip From Hell

"Alan" was flying to New York for a massive conference.

He was stressed. His Right Nostril (Sun) was stuck open (Solar Overload).

His flight was at 6:00 AM.

He rushed out of the house.

He stepped out with his Left Foot (Mismatch - Sun breath requires Right foot).

He was traveling East (Good direction for Sun), but he failed the First Step.

The Cascade:

Because he stepped with the "Empty Leg," he tripped slightly on the curb. Nothing major, just a stumble.

But the "Wobble" was in his system.

At the airport, he realized he forgot his noise-canceling headphones (Air element chaos creeping in due to misalignment).

He was irritable (Solar). He got into an argument with the TSA agent.

He was "randomly selected" for a search. Delay.

He barely made the flight.

On the plane, the seatback screen was broken.

He arrived in NY exhausted, angry, and ungrounded.

The Correction:

If Alan had paused at the door:

1. **Audit:** Right Nostril Open.
2. **Action:** Step **Right Foot** first.
3. **Mindset:** "I am Solar. I am commanding this journey."

He would have moved with precision. He would have checked his bag (Solar logic). He would have been polite but firm with TSA.

The "First Step" sets the timeline. Alan stepped onto the "Chaos Timeline" because he ignored the launch protocol.

Part Vii: Advanced Protocol – The "Prana Breath" (Inhaling The Destination)

There is a mystic technique for ensure safety when entering a dangerous territory (e.g., a bad neighborhood, a courtroom, or a difficult country).

It involves Inhaling the Direction.

The Theory:

By inhaling from the direction you are going, you "taste" the energy of that place and integrate it before you arrive. You make yourself "local" before you get there.

The Technique:

1. Face the direction of travel.
2. Check which nostril is active. (e.g., Right).
3. Turn your head slightly so the **Active Nostril** is "scooping" the air from that direction.
4. Inhale deeply. Visualize the essence of the destination entering your body and merging with your Prana.
5. Exhale.
6. Repeat 3 times.
7. **Step out.**

Why it works:

It creates Resonance. You are telling your bio-field: "I am already one with this place. I am not an invader; I am a guest."

The environment tends to treat you more kindly.

Part Viii: Somatic Lab – The Threshold Drill

We are going to practice the launch.

You don't need to go anywhere. Just practice the exit.

Exercise: The Perfect Exit

1. **Stand at your bedroom door.** Close it.
2. **The Pause:** Put your hand on the knob. Feel the metal. Stop.
3. **The Check:** Finger under nose. Which side is Purna (Full)?
    - *Assume Right/Sun.*
4. **The Weight Shift:** Shift your body weight onto your **Left Leg.**
    - *Why?* To free up the **Right Leg** for the step.

5. **The Breath:** Inhale deeply through the Right.
6. **The Step:** Open the door. Swing the **Right Leg** forward. Land firmly. Exhale.
7. **The Walk:** Walk 5 steps with authority.

The Feeling:

Notice how "Solid" that first step felt.

Notice how you didn't look down.

Notice the sense of Forward Drive.

Compare this to your usual "stumble out of bed" routine.

The difference is Royalty.

Part Ix: Summary – The Traveler's Checklist

VARIABLE	CHECK	RULE	CORRECTION
THE LAUNCH	Which Breath?	**Step with Active Foot.**	Stop. Shift weight. Re-step.
THE DIRECTION	Which Way?	**Sun = East/ North. Moon = West/ South.**	**Pivot Hack:** Walk 7 steps in the correct direction, then turn.
THE ELEMENT	What Shape?	**Earth/Water = Go. Air/Fire = Caution.**	Wait 20 mins for element shift.
THE VOID	Equal Breath?	**STOP.**	**Do not leave.** Wait for flow.

Conclusion:

You are now a Master of Displacement.

You know how to leave the house like a King.

You know how to navigate the magnetic currents of the city.

But...

What if you are not going somewhere?

What if you are looking for something?

What if something has gone missing?

- "Where are my keys?"
- "Where is my wallet?"
- "Did the thief go North or South?"

The breath is not just a compass for travel; it is a Radar for Lost Objects.

The ancient science of Nashta Jataka (Astrology of Loss) uses the breath to triangulate the location of missing items.

In Sub-Chapter 3.3, we become Detectives.

We will learn why a "Moon Breath" means the object is near water or fabric.

We will learn why a "Sun Breath" means the object is near metal or height.

And we will learn how to find what was lost.

Turn the page. The search begins.

3.3: Finding the Lost – The Pranic Radar

> "When the question is asked: 'Where is the object?', look to the Breath. If the Sun flows, it is high and to the East. If the Moon flows, it is low and to the West. If the breath is Empty, the object has crossed the river of no return."
>
> — Shiva Swarodaya, Verses 215-220

Panic.

It is the feeling of patting your pocket and finding nothing.

It is the cold drop in your stomach when you realize your wallet, your wedding ring, or your child is not where they are supposed to be.

When we lose something, our instinct is Chaos.

We run around. We check the same drawer three times. We scream. We blame.

We generate massive amounts of Air Element (Vayu) anxiety, which actually hides the object further because Air creates confusion.

The Swara Yogi does not panic.

The Swara Yogi freezes.

He knows that the object has not ceased to exist. It is simply in a coordinate of space that he cannot currently see.

But his nervous system can see it.

Because the Prana in his body is connected to the Prana of the Universe, and the Universe knows exactly where the keys are.

This sub-chapter is about Nashta Prashna (The Question of the Lost).

We are going to turn your body into a metal detector.

We are going to learn why a Solar Breath means the object is near the ceiling or the stove.

We are going to learn why a Lunar Breath means the object is under the bed or near the sink.

And we are going to learn the harsh truth: Sometimes, the breath tells you to stop looking, because the object is gone for good.

Part I: The Mechanics Of Triangulation – The Questioner's Vector

To find an object, you need a Reference Point.

In traditional astrology, the Reference Point is the Time.

In Swara Yoga, the Reference Point is Position.

Scenario:

Someone comes to you and asks: "Where is my ring?"

Or, you ask yourself: "Where is my ring?"

The Variables:

1. **The Nostril:** Which breath is active? (Sun vs. Moon).
2. **The Position:** Where is the questioner standing relative to you? (Or if you are asking yourself, which direction are you facing?).
3. **The Element:** What is the shape/taste of the breath?

The First Law of Radar:

> *"The answer lies in the direction of the Flow."*

If the question comes from the Purna (Full) side, the object is recoverable. It is "alive" in your field.

If the question comes from the Shunya (Empty) side, the object is unrecoverable. It has entered the Void. It is likely stolen or destroyed.

Example:

Your spouse runs in. "I lost my car keys!"

You check your nose. Right Nostril (Sun) is flowing.

Your spouse is standing on your Right Side (Purna).

Verdict: Found. The keys are safe. They are nearby. We just need to calculate the coordinates.

If your spouse was standing on your Left Side (Shunya/Empty) while you had a Solar breath...

Verdict: Lost. The keys might be stolen, dropped down a drain, or taken by someone who won't give them back. The energy connection is broken.

Part Ii: The Solar Search – High, Hard, And East

> *"If the Sun flows, seek the object in the East or North. It lies in places of fire, metal, or height. It is not hidden deep; it is in plain sight but overlooked."*

The Compass:

If Right Nostril (Pingala) is active, the object has gravitated toward Solar Directions:

- **East:** The direction of sunrise.
- **North:** The direction of power.

The Altitude:

Solar energy rises. Heat goes up.

Therefore, the object is likely High Up.

- On a shelf.

- On top of the fridge.
- In the attic.
- In the upstairs bedroom.

The Environment (Fire/Metal):

The Sun rules Fire and hardness. Look near:

- **Heat Sources:** The oven, the fireplace, the heater, the radiator.
- **Electronics:** Near the TV, the computer, the charging station.
- **Bright Places:** Near a window, under a lamp.
- **Hard Surfaces:** On a marble counter, a metal table, a concrete floor.

The Psychology of the Loss:

Solar loss is usually due to Haste.

You put it down quickly while rushing to do something else. You didn't "hide" it; you "abandoned" it in motion.

It is likely sitting right out in the open, but your eyes are moving too fast to see it.

Prediction:

"It is in the East room (Kitchen/Office). Look up. Look near the lights or the electronics. It is visible."

Part Iii: The Lunar Search – Low, Soft, And West

> *"If the Moon flows, seek the object in the West or South. It lies in places of water, cloth, or depth. It is hidden, buried, or wrapped."*

The Compass:

If Left Nostril (Ida) is active, the object has gravitated toward Lunar Directions:

- **West:** The direction of sunset.
- **South:** The direction of rest/ancestors.

The Altitude:

Lunar energy descends. Water flows down.

Therefore, the object is likely Low Down.

- Under the bed.
- In the basement.
- On the floor.
- Buried in a bag.

The Environment (Water/Cloth):

The Moon rules Water and softness. Look near:

- **Water Sources:** The bathroom, the sink, the laundry room, near a vase.
- **Soft Places:** In a pile of clothes, inside a pocket, under a cushion, in the bedsheets.
- **Dark Places:** In a drawer, in a closet, somewhere "cozy."

The Psychology of the Loss:

Lunar loss is usually due to Absent-Mindedness or Comfort.

You were daydreaming. You put it in your pocket. You fell asleep with it.

It is likely "wrapped" in something. It is hidden.

Prediction:

"It is in the West room (Bedroom/Bathroom). Look down. Shake out the clothes. Look under the sofa cushions. It is buried."

Part Iv: The Elemental Refinement – Forensic Detail

We can get more specific.

Once you know the Side (Sun/Moon), check the Element (Mirror/Finger/Taste).

This tells you the nature of the hiding spot.

1. Earth (Square Breath / Sweet Taste)

- **Location:** On the ground. Under something heavy. In a garden. In a stone or ceramic container.
- **Status: Very Safe.** It hasn't moved. It is exactly where you left it.
- **Prediction:** "Look on the floor, under the heaviest furniture."

2. Water (Crescent Breath / Astringent Taste)

- **Location:** Near liquids. Bathroom, kitchen sink, near a pool. Or inside a liquid container (did you drop the ring in a drink?).
- **Status: Safe but hidden.** It might be wet.
- **Prediction:** "Check the bathroom counter or the laundry pile."

3. Fire (Triangle Breath / Bitter Taste)

- **Location:** Near electronics, stove, fireplace, or in the garage (engine heat). Or in a place of conflict (lawyer's office, police station).
- **Status: Damaged?** Check if it is broken or scratched.
- **Prediction:** "Check the kitchen or near the computer."

4. Air (Circle Breath / Sour Taste)

- **Location:** Outside. In the car. On a balcony. Near a fan or window.
- **Status: Moving.** Someone might have picked it up and moved it. Or it blew away.
- **Prediction:** "It is not in its usual place. It has migrated. Check your car or coat pockets (travel items)."

5. Ether (Void Breath / No Taste)

- **Location:** Nowhere.
- **Status: Gone.**
- **Prediction:** "Stop looking."

Part V: The "Empty" Verdict – When To Give Up

This is the hardest part to accept.

If you ask the question, and the breath is Shunya (Blocked/ Empty) relative to the direction of the query, or if the Element is Ether...

The object is lost.

- **Scenario:** "Where is my wallet?"
- **Breath:** Left Nostril flowing.
- **Query:** You are facing **East** (Solar direction).
- **Analysis:** You are looking into the "Empty Direction" (Left breath empowers West, but you are facing East).
- **Result:** You are facing a Void.
- **Meaning:** The wallet was stolen. Or it fell into a place where it cannot be retrieved (e.g., down a sewer grate).

The Mercy of the No:

Knowing it is lost is a gift. It stops the panic loop.

You can stop searching and start canceling your credit cards.

Swara Yoga saves you time, even in failure.

Part Vi: Case Study – The Lost Wedding Ring

"Julia" lost her diamond ring. She was hysterical. She tore the house apart.

She called me.

"Stop," I said. "Where are you standing?"

"In the kitchen."

"Face North. Take a breath. Tell me which nostril is open."

She checked. "My Left Nostril is very open. It feels cool."

"Okay. Left Nostril = Moon."

The Analysis:

- **Nostril:** Moon (Ida).
- **Direction: West/South**.
- **Height: Low**.
- **Environment: Soft/Water**.

"Julia, do not look in the kitchen (Fire/East). Go to the West side of the house. What room is there?"

"The Master Bedroom and Bath."

"Okay. It is Low and Soft. Look in the bedsheets, the laundry hamper, or near the bathtub."

She ran to the bedroom.

Ten minutes later, she texted me a photo.

The ring was inside the pocket of her bathrobe (Soft/Cloth), which was lying on the floor (Low) in the bathroom (Water/West).

If she had continued looking in the kitchen (Solar), she never would have found it. The breath pointed the compass.

Part Vii: Advanced Technique – The "Dowsing" Breath

What if you don't know the room?

You can use your breath as a real-time Geiger Counter.

The Protocol:

1. **Stand in the center of the house.**
2. **Calibrate:** Check which nostril is active. (e.g., Right).
3. The Scan:
   Turn your body slowly in a circle.
   Face East. Take a breath.
   Face South. Take a breath.
   Face West. Take a breath.
   Face North. Take a breath.
4. The Signal:
   Notice where the breath feels Strongest and Smoothest.
   Even if your Right nostril is open, it will flow better when you face the direction of the object.
   It feels like a "magnetic click." The air rushes in easier.
   When you face the wrong direction, the breath feels subtle resistance or "static."
5. The Hunt:
   Walk in the direction of the strongest flow.
   Repeat the scan in that room.

Why it works:

You are entrained with the object. Your subconscious mind knows where it is (because your subconscious records everything). It is guiding your autonomic nervous system to signal "Hot" or "Cold" through the breath.

Part Viii: Summary – The Radar Checklist

VARIABLE	IF SUN (RIGHT) FLOWS	IF MOON (LEFT) FLOWS
Direction	East / North	West / South
Height	High (Eye level or	Low (Floor level,

	above)	under things)
Texture	Hard, Metal, Hot, Bright	Soft, Cloth, Damp, Dark
Recovery	Quick retrieval. Visible.	Slow retrieval. Hidden/Buried.
Status (Empty Side)	Stolen / Irretrievable.	Lost / Washed away.

Conclusion of Chapter 3:

You have mastered the Compass.

You know how to position yourself for power (Sub-Chapter 3.1).

You know how to launch a journey (Sub-Chapter 3.2).

You know how to find the lost (Sub-Chapter 3.3).

But the world is not just made of Space. It is made of Sound.

Names have power.

- "Should I hire **R**obert or **S**arah?"
- "Should I name the company **A**pex or **Z**enith?"

The first letter of a name carries an Elemental Frequency.

If you hire a "Fire Name" during a "Water Breath," you create steam (conflict).

If you hire an "Earth Name" during an "Earth Breath," you create a mountain (success).

In Chapter 4: Phonetical Astrology, we decode the alphabet.

We will learn Matrika Shastra—the science of sound.

We will learn why some names sound "lucky" to you and others sound "wrong."

And we will learn to predict the outcome of a partnership simply by hearing the person's name.

Turn the page. The Oracle is about to speak.

CHAPTER 4: PHONETICAL ASTROLOGY (THE SOUND OF REALITY)

4.1: The Alphabet of Elements – The Matrika Code

> "The Universe was born from Sound (Nada). The letters are the Mothers (Matrikas) of all creation. He who knows the Element of the First Letter knows the destiny of the Name. Do not ask 'Who is he?' Ask 'What is his sound?'"
>
> — Shiva Swarodaya, Verses 225-230

What is in a name?

To the modern mind, a name is just a tag. A social convenience.

"I am John." "This is Apple." "That is a table."

We think names are arbitrary labels stuck onto objects like price tags.

But the Swara Yogi knows better.

In the Tantric worldview, Sound precedes Matter.

The universe vibrates before it solidifies. The vibration creates the form.

Therefore, the Name is not a label; it is the Blueprint.

The sound "KA" has a different geometry, density, and impact on the nervous system than the sound "RA."

One is a square (Earth). The other is a triangle (Fire).

When you name a company, a child, or a project, you are choosing its Elemental Frequency.

- If you name a company with a **Fire Letter**, it will be aggressive, fast, and prone to conflict.
- If you name it with a **Water Letter**, it will be fluid, popular, and unstable.

This is the science of Phonetical Astrology (Akshara Jyotish).

You do not need a birth chart to know if a person will be stubborn or flighty. You just need to hear the first syllable of their name.

In this sub-chapter, we are going to decode the Alphabet.

We are going to learn why the vowels (Swaras) are the Soul and the consonants (Vyanjanas) are the Body.

We are going to classify every sound you can make into the Five Elements.

And you will never hear a name the same way again. You will hear the Tattvas speaking.

Part I: The Metaphysics Of Sound – Vak Shakti

To understand this, you must accept a premise from Quantum Physics: Everything is Frequency.

Your vocal cords are an instrument that shapes air into geometric waves.

When you say a name, you are firing a specific waveform into the brain of the listener.

The "Matrika" (Little Mother):

In Sanskrit, letters are called Matrikas, meaning "Little Mothers."

Why? Because they give birth to reality.

Each letter is a deity. It has a personality. It has a Shakti (Power).

The First Letter Rule:

The Shiva Swarodaya focuses primarily on the First Letter (or First Syllable) of a name.

Why the first?

Because the Attack (the initial sound) sets the trajectory.

It is like the "First Step" in travel. The initial burst of energy defines the inertia of the word.

If a name starts with "K" (Hard, Guttural), it hits the air with an explosive, grounding force.

If a name starts with "S" (Soft, Sibilant), it slides into the air with a fluid, airy force.

The Application:

We are going to use this to predict Compatibility and Outcome.

- "Will **K**evin and **S**arah get along?"
- "Will Project Titan succeed?"
  The answer lies in the elemental friction or harmony between the sounds.

Part Ii: The Two Wings – Swara (Vowels) Vs. Vyanjana (Consonants)

The alphabet is divided into two kingdoms.

1. The Swaras (Vowels): The Soul

- **Sounds:** A, E, I, O, U (and the Sanskrit variations like Aa, Ee, etc.).
- **Nature: Shiva** (Consciousness).
- **Function:** Vowels can be spoken without obstruction. You can sing "Ahhhhh" forever. They are continuous. They represent the **Life Force (Prana)**.
- **The Oracle:** A name starting with a Vowel (e.g., *Adam, Oliver, Isabella*) is ruled by **Spirit/Air**.
  - *Vibe:* Independent, intellectual, spiritual, hard to pin down.
  - *Power:* They provide the "Life" to the Consonants.

2. The Vyanjanas (Consonants): The Body

- **Sounds:** K, T, P, M, R, etc.

- **Nature: Shakti** (Matter).
- **Function:** Consonants cannot be spoken without a vowel helper (you can't say "K" without a subtle "uh" or "a" after it). They act as **Stops** or **Structures**.
- **The Oracle:** A name starting with a Consonant (e.g., *David, Robert, Kate*) is ruled by **Matter/Form**.
    - *Vibe:* Grounded, worldly, structured, defined.
    - *Power:* They provide the "Shape" to the Spirit.

The Swara Insight:

Most practical questions ("Will I get money?", "Will I win?") are Consonant questions. They deal with matter.

Therefore, we focus heavily on the Consonant Groups (Vargas) to determine the elemental nature of worldly things.

Part Iii: The Periodic Table Of Sound – The 5 Vargas

The Sanskrit alphabet organizes consonants by where they are spoken in the mouth.

This is not random. It traces the movement of energy from the throat (Guttural) to the lips (Labial).

This progression maps perfectly to the Five Elements.

Here is the Master Code.

(Note: English names act as approximations. Use the sound, not the spelling. "Ph" in Philip is an "F" sound. "Ch" in Chris is a "K" sound).

Group 1: The Gutturals (Ka-Varga) – THE EARTH ELEMENT

- **Sounds: K, Kh, G, Gh, Ng** (Hard G like "Go").
- **Point of Origin:** The Throat (Root of the tongue). Deepest sound.
- **Element: Earth (Prithvi).**

- **Planet: Mars / Mercury** (Context dependent, often Mars for hardness).
- **The Vibe:** Hard. Fixed. Explosive. Grounding.
- **Names:** *Kate, Gary, Kevin, Greg, Chloe (Hard K sound).*
- **The Prediction:**
    - **Stability:** High.
    - **Speed:** Slow but unstoppable.
    - **Nature:** Stubborn, practical, materialistic, reliable.
    - **Best For:** Construction, banking, long-term foundations.
    - **Worst For:** Diplomacy, flexibility.

Group 2: The Palatals (Cha-Varga) – THE WATER ELEMENT

- **Sounds: Ch, Chh, J, Jh, Ny** (Soft J like "Joy", Ch like "Chat").
- **Point of Origin:** The Hard Palate (Tongue touches roof).
- **Element: Water (Jala).**
- **Planet: Venus / Moon.**
- **The Vibe:** Fluid. Connecting. Sticky. Emotional.
- **Names:** *James, Jessica, Charlie, Julia, George (Soft G).*
- **The Prediction:**
    - **Flow:** High.
    - **Emotion:** Deep.
    - **Nature:** Social, artistic, persuasive, romantic, adaptable.
    - **Best For:** Sales, networking, arts, relationships.
    - **Worst For:** Rigid discipline, isolation.

Group 3: The Cerebrals/Retroflex (Ta-Varga) – THE FIRE ELEMENT

- **Sounds: T, Th, D, Dh, N** (Hard T/D sounds).
- *Note:* In English, T and D are often softer (Dental), but for Swara purposes, we group the "Sharp" consonants here.
- **Point of Origin:** The Roof of the mouth (Tongue curls back).
- **Element: Fire (Agni).**
- **Planet: Sun / Mars.**

- **The Vibe:** Sharp. Cutting. Direct. Penetrating.
- **Names:** *Tom, David, Teresa, Daniel, Tyler.*
- **The Prediction:**
    - **Energy:** High / Hot.
    - **Conflict:** Likely.
    - **Nature:** Ambitious, logical, aggressive, decisive, transformative.
    - **Best For:** Leadership, litigation, surgery, innovation.
    - **Worst For:** Peacemaking, patience.

Group 4: The Labials (Pa-Varga) – THE AIR ELEMENT

- **Sounds: P, Ph, B, Bh, M** (Sounds made with the Lips).
- **Point of Origin:** The Lips. The most external sound.
- **Element: Air (Vayu).**
- **Planet: Saturn.**
- **The Vibe:** Mobile. Dispersive. Communicative.
- **Names:** *Peter, Paul, Mary, Ben, Mike, Philip.*
- **The Prediction:**
    - **Movement:** Constant.
    - **Stability:** Low.
    - **Nature:** Intellectual, communicative, travel-prone, ungrounded.
    - **Best For:** Media, travel, logistics, change.
    - **Worst For:** Secrets, stillness.

Group 5: The Semivowels (Ya-Varga) – THE ETHER ELEMENT

- **Sounds: Y, R, L, V, S, Sh, H.**
- *Note:* This group is a mix. In advanced Tantra, they have specific elements (R=Fire, V=Water, L=Earth, Y=Air, H=Ether). But in the simplified **Varga System** of *Shiva Swarodaya*, the non-stop consonants are often treated as the "Space" or **Ether** group because they bridge the gap between vowel and consonant.
- **Element: Ether (Akasha)** (with elemental sub-tones).
- **The Vibe:** Spiritual. Vast. Complex.
- **Names:** *Sarah, Harry, Larry, Ryan, William.*

- **The Prediction:**
  - **Nature:** Mysterious, spiritual, expansive, hard to define.
  - **Result:** Often mixed or dependent on the *second* letter.

Part Iv: The Predictive Profiles – Naming Your Destiny

Knowing the Element of a name allows you to predict the "Flavor" of the interaction.

The Earth Name (K, G):

- *Scenario:* You are hiring a CFO.
- *Candidate A:* **Kevin** (Earth).
- *Candidate B:* **Paul** (Air).
- *The Oracle:* Hire Kevin. A CFO needs stability (Earth). Paul (Air) will be creative but might lose the receipts or change the system too often.

The Fire Name (T, D):

- *Scenario:* You need a divorce lawyer.
- *Candidate A:* **David** (Fire).
- *Candidate B:* **Mary** (Air/Water vibe).
- *The Oracle:* Hire David. Fire cuts. You need a sword. Mary might be too soft or scattered.

The Water Name (Ch, J):

- *Scenario:* You want a romantic partner.
- *Candidate:* **Julia** (Water).
- *The Oracle:* Excellent. Water rules connection. Expect emotion and flow.

The Air Name (P, B, M):

- *Scenario:* You want a travel buddy.
- *Candidate:* **Mike** (Air).

- *The Oracle:* Perfect. Air loves movement. The trip will be dynamic. Do not hire him to guard a fortress (too restless).

Part V: The Vowel Anomaly – The Spirit Names

What about names starting with **A, E, I, O, U**?

- Examples: Alice, Eric, Oliver.
  These are Pure Spirit names.
  They are not bound by the heavy elements of Earth or Water.
  They are Etheric by nature.

Prediction:

- **Pros:** Highly intelligent, adaptable, often visionary. They can channel any element they choose.
- **Cons:** Hard to ground. They can be "floaty." In a business partnership, they need a Consonant Partner (Earth/Fire) to anchor them.
- *Compatibility:* An "Alice" (Spirit) works well with a "Gary" (Earth) – Spirit infuses Matter.

Part Vi: The Somatic Lab – The Name Resonance Test

We are going to test the vibration of names in your own body.

This is how you feel the Element.

Exercise: The Mantra of Names

1. **Sit quietly.** Close your eyes.
2. **The Earth Test:**
   - Say the sound **"KA"** repeatedly. *Ka... Ka... Ka...*
   - Focus on *where* it hits. (Back of throat).
   - *Feel:* Does it feel hard? abrupt? Does it stop the breath?
   - *Visualize:* A stone hitting the ground.

3. **The Water Test:**
    - Say the sound **"JA"** repeatedly. *Ja... Ja... Ja...*
    - Focus on the palate.
    - *Feel:* Does it feel softer? wetter?
    - *Visualize:* A splash.
4. **The Fire Test:**
    - Say the sound **"TA"** repeatedly. *Ta... Ta... Ta...*
    - Focus on the roof of the mouth.
    - *Feel:* Is it sharp? percussive?
    - *Visualize:* A spark or a hammer strike.
5. **The Air Test:**
    - Say the sound **"PA"** repeatedly. *Pa... Pa... Pa...*
    - Focus on the lips.
    - *Feel:* It pushes air *out*. It is explosive but light.
    - *Visualize:* A bubble bursting.

The Application:

Now say the name of your partner or boss.

Which sound is dominant?

Does their personality match the Element?

(90% of the time, it does. Nomen est Omen – Name is Destiny).

Part Vii: Advanced Strategy – Altering The Name

What if your name has the "Wrong Element"?

- *Scenario:* You are a "Paul" (Air) but you want to be a stable banker (Earth).
- *Problem:* Your name vibrates with instability.

The Hack:

You don't need to legally change your name.

Change the Nickname.

Adopt a nickname that starts with the desired Element.

- Paul -> **G**reg (No, that's weird).
- Paul -> **C**aptain (Earth/Hard C).
- Paul -> **T**iger (Fire).

Or, simply emphasize the Last Name if it has a better element.

If Paul's last name is King (Earth), go by "King."

By changing the sound you answer to, you change the frequency you vibrate at.

Summary: The Alphabetical Almanac

VARGA (Group)	SOUNDS	ELEMENT	QUALITY	BEST FOR
Gutturals	K, G, Kh, Gh	**EARTH**	Stable, Hard	Business, Assets, Loyalty
Palatals	Ch, J, Sh	**WATER**	Fluid, Social	Arts, Love, Sales
Cerebrals	T, D, Th	**FIRE**	Sharp, Hot	War, Law, Leadership
Labials	P, B, M	**AIR**	Mobile, Light	Travel, Media, Change
Semivowels	Y, R, L, V, H	**ETHER/MIX**	Spiritual	Ideas, Vision, Spirit

Conclusion:

You now see the matrix code.

Names are not random. They are elemental assignments.

When you meet a "Kevin," you are meeting a piece of Earth.

When you meet a "David," you are meeting a piece of Fire.

But knowing the Element of the Name is just the first step.

The real magic happens when you combine the Name with the Breath.

- What happens when a "Fire Name" asks you a question

while your "Water Breath" is flowing?

- What happens when an "Earth Name" asks you for money while your "Air Breath" is flowing?

This is Dynamic Compatibility.

This is how you predict the outcome of a meeting the moment the person introduces themselves.

In Sub-Chapter 4.2, we will learn the Solar and Lunar Letters.

We will learn the "Resonance Rule."

And we will learn why you should never say "Yes" to a "Solar Name" when your "Lunar Breath" is active.

Turn the page. The conversation is about to start.

4.2: The Solar and Lunar Letters – The Acoustic Charge

> "The Letters are not equal. Some are born of the Sun; they burn and cut. Some are born of the Moon; they cool and bind. If a Solar Name enters a Lunar Breath, it is like fire hitting water—steam, fog, and confusion. But if Fire meets Fire, there is Light."
>
> — Shiva Swarodaya, Verses 235-240

We have learned that letters have Elements (Earth, Water, Fire, Air, Ether).

But there is a simpler, more immediate binary code hidden in the alphabet: Temperature.

Every sound you make creates friction in the vocal tract.

- Some sounds are **Hard (Kathora)**. They require force. They hit the teeth and the roof of the mouth. They generate heat. These are **Solar**.
- Some sounds are **Soft (Mridu)**. They glide. They use the lips and the soft palate. They generate flow. These are **Lunar**.

Why does this matter?

Because you are constantly interacting with names.

- You get an email from **R**ichard.
- You swipe right on **S**arah.
- You interview **T**om.

If your breath is currently Lunar (Left), and you interact with Richard (Solar Name), you are creating a Dissonance Field.

His name carries a frequency of "Heat/Action," but your receiver is set to "Cool/Reception."

The result? Misunderstanding. Friction. A feeling that he is "too aggressive" or you are "too passive."

But if you interact with Richard while your Solar (Right) breath is flowing... SNAP.

Resonance.

You "get" him. He respects you. The deal closes instantly.

This sub-chapter is about Acoustic Compatibility.

We are going to classify the alphabet into Sun and Moon.

We are going to learn the Resonance Rule (Match the Name to the Breath).

And we are going to learn why you should never sign a contract with a "Solar Name" when you are in a "Lunar Mood."

Part I: The Physics Of Hard And Soft – Classifying The Alphabet

To determine if a name is Solar or Lunar, we look at the Phonetic Pressure.

Does the sound "punch" the air? Or does it "caress" the air?

1. The Solar Letters (The Sword)

> *"The Sun rules the hard consonants. They are the seeds of power."*

Solar letters are percussive. They require a sudden release of air pressure. They often involve the tongue striking a hard surface (teeth or roof of mouth).

- **The Sounds:**
  - **K** (Kevin, Kate)
  - **T** (Tom, Tyler) - *Hard T*
  - **D** (David, Dan) - *Hard D*
  - **R** (Robert, Rachel) - *The Roaring R*
  - **G** (Gary, Greg) - *Hard G*
  - **J** (Jack, James) - *When pronounced hard*

- **The Vibe:**
  - **Male / Yang / Pingala.**
  - These names carry a charge of **Leadership, Aggression, and Logic**.
  - They project outward. They demand attention.
  - *Note on 'R':* The sound 'Ra' is the seed sound of Fire (*Agni*). Names starting with R are intensely Solar. They burn obstacles but can also cause conflict.

2. The Lunar Letters (The Shield)

> *"The Moon rules the soft consonants and the sibilants. They are the seeds of attraction."*

Lunar letters are continuous or soft. They allow air to flow over the tongue without a violent stop. They often involve the lips or the soft palate.

- **The Sounds:**
  - **S** (Sarah, Sam)
  - **Sh** (Sheila, Shane)
  - **M** (Mary, Mike)
  - **N** (Nancy, Nathan)
  - **L** (Larry, Lisa)
  - **V / W** (Victoria, William)
  - **Ch** (Charlie, Chelsea) - *Soft Ch*
  - **H** (Harry, Hannah) - *The Breath Sound*
- **The Vibe:**
  - **Female / Yin / Ida.**
  - These names carry a charge of **Connection, Flow, and Healing**.
  - They draw people in. They are magnetic.
  - *Note on 'S':* The sound 'Sa' is the seed of Shakti/Moon. Names starting with S are fluid and adaptive.

3. The Vowels (The Spirit) – The Special Case

- **Sounds:** A, E, I, O, U (Adam, Eric, Ivy).
- **Classification:** Generally **Lunar/Neutral**.
- **Why:** Vowels are pure breath. They have no "obstruction."

They are the most receptive sounds.

- **Rule:** Treat Vowel Names as **Lunar** unless they are followed immediately by a hard consonant (e.g., **Ar**thur = Solar influence due to R). But purely vowel-led names (Oliver, Alice) are Soft.

Part Ii: The Prediction Rule – The Law Of Resonance

> *"When the Breath matches the Name, the fruit falls into the hand without effort."*

This is the core technique of Phonetical Astrology.

You don't need to know the person's horoscope. You just need to know their Name and your Breath.

The Equation:

Name Charge + Your Breath Charge = Outcome.

Scenario A: Perfect Solar Resonance (The Power Move)

- **The Name:** Robert (Solar).
- **Your Breath: Right Nostril** (Solar) is flowing.
- **The Chemistry:** Fire meets Fire.
- **The Prediction: Instant Success.**
  - **Business:** You will agree on terms quickly. The energy is high. Decisions are made fast.
  - **Relationship:** Passionate, dynamic, "Power Couple" energy.
  - **Conflict:** If you are fighting, it will be a "Clean War." The stronger person wins quickly. No passive-aggressive lingering.
- **Why:** You are vibrating at the same frequency. There is zero

translation loss.

Scenario B: Perfect Lunar Resonance (The Soul Connection)

- **The Name:** Sarah (Lunar).
- **Your Breath: Left Nostril** (Lunar) is flowing.
- **The Chemistry:** Water meets Water.
- **The Prediction: Deep Flow.**
    - **Business:** Trust is established. It feels like a partnership, not a transaction.
    - **Relationship:** Emotional intimacy. You feel "safe" with this person.
    - **Conflict:** Conflict dissolves. You talk it out. Empathy rules.
- **Why:** You are both in the "Receiving" mode. You are listening to each other.

Part Iii: The Dissonance Rule – The Law Of Friction

> *"When the Breath opposes the Name, the path is blocked by thorns. The Solar Name burns the Lunar Breath. The Lunar Name drowns the Solar Breath."*

This is where deals die and dates go wrong.

Mismatch = Friction.

Scenario C: The Scorched Earth (Solar Name + Lunar Breath)

- **The Name:** Tom (Solar).
- **Your Breath: Left Nostril** (Lunar) is flowing.
- **The Chemistry:** Fire hitting Water.
- **The Experience:**
    - You feel **overwhelmed**. Tom seems too loud, too pushy, or "too much."
    - You try to connect emotionally (Lunar), but he responds with logic (Solar).
    - You feel drained because your "Cool" system is trying

to process his "Hot" signal.

- **The Prediction: Delay or Rejection.**
  - You will likely say "No" because he feels unsafe to your nervous system.
  - Or, you will sign the deal but regret it later because you felt pressured.

Scenario D: The Damp Squib (Lunar Name + Solar Breath)

- **The Name:** Lisa (Lunar).
- **Your Breath: Right Nostril** (Solar) is flowing.
- **The Chemistry:** Water hitting Fire.
- **The Experience:**
  - You feel **impatient**. Lisa seems slow, vague, or "weak."
  - You want to get to the point (Solar), but she wants to build rapport (Lunar).
  - You might steamroll her. You dominate the conversation.
- **The Prediction: Unsatisfying Victory.**
  - You might get what you want, but you won't respect her.
  - The partnership will fail because you will eventually view her as a drag on your speed.

Part Iv: Strategic Matching – How To Hack The Meeting

Now that you know the rules, you can game the system.

You have a meeting with David (Solar Name).

You check your nose. You are breathing Left (Lunar).

Danger: Mismatch imminent.

The Strategy:
You have two choices:

1. **Switch the Breath (Bio-Hack):**

- Use the **Fist Hack** (Chapter 5) to force the **Right Nostril** open.
- *Result:* You match his frequency. You meet David as an equal. Fire meets Fire. The deal happens.

2. **Switch the Frame (Judo):**
    - If you *cannot* switch the breath (e.g., stuck in Lunar Overload), you must change the *nature* of the interaction.
    - Do not try to "out-alpha" David.
    - Use your Lunar state to **absorb** him. Let him talk. Let him burn his energy out. Be the water that cools the steel.
    - *Result:* He feels heard. He feels soothed. You win by yielding.

The "Name-Drop" Hack:

If you need to trigger a specific state in yourself, say a name repeatedly.

- Need to wake up? Chant **RAM** (Solar seed sound).
- Need to calm down? Chant **SOM** (Lunar seed sound).
- Sound affects *your* physiology too.

Part V: The Vowel Anomaly – The Soft Opening

Names starting with vowels (Adam, Elizabeth, Olivia) are special.

They are Etheric / Lunar.

They require a Soft Approach.

The Vowel Rule:

- **Never approach a Vowel Name with a Raging Solar Breath.**
    - If you come at an "Oliver" with high-intensity Right Nostril aggression, you will spook him. He will ghost

you. Vowel names value freedom and space (Ether). Solar energy feels like a cage to them.

- **The Fix:** Always switch to **Left Nostril (Moon)** before calling a Vowel Name.
    - Create space. Be receptive. Let them come to you.

Exception:

If the vowel is followed by a hard stop (e.g., Ex-avier, Ac-tion), treat it as a mix. But generally, Vowels = Moon.

Part VI: Case Studies – The Oracle in Action
Case Study 1: The Failed Partnership

"John" (Solar - Hard J) and "Mary" (Lunar - Soft M) were trying to start a business.

They fought constantly.

John complained: "She's too slow. She's indecisive." (Solar judging Lunar).

Mary complained: "He's a bully. He doesn't listen." (Lunar judging Solar).

The Swara Diagnosis:

They were holding their meetings in the morning.

John (Solar Name) was waking up Solar. (Hyper-Solar).

Mary (Lunar Name) was waking up Lunar. (Hyper-Lunar).

They were operating at opposite ends of the spectrum. Maximum Dissonance.

The Intervention:

I told them: "Only meet when your breaths are switched."

- John had to force his **Left Nostril** (Moon) to activate his empathy.
- Mary had to force her **Right Nostril** (Sun) to activate her assertiveness.

- When they met in this "Artificial Cross-State," they met in the middle. John softened. Mary sharpened.
- They built a multimillion-dollar company.

Case Study 2: The Sales Call

"Ben" (Air/Lunar) was trying to sell to a client named "Karl" (Earth/Solar - Hard K).

Ben kept pitching "Innovation, flexibility, change" (Air values).

Karl kept saying "No."

Ben checked his breath. He was Left (Moon).

He was trying to sell Air/Water to a Rock (Karl).

The Pivot:

Ben used the Fist Hack. Switched to Right Nostril (Sun).

He changed his language. He stopped saying "flexible." He started saying "Solid. Guaranteed. ROI. Structure." (Solar/Earth words).

He matched Karl's frequency.

Karl signed immediately. "Finally," Karl said, "Some concrete numbers."

Part Vii: Somatic Lab – The Name Taste Test

You need to feel the weight of names in your mouth.

Exercise: The Phonetic Weighing Scale

1. **Sit comfortably.**
2. **The Solar Test:**
   - Say the name **"GREG"**.
   - Feel the back of your throat constrict. Feel the stoppage of air. Feel the "thud."
   - *Sensation:* Heavy, hot, abrupt.

   - *Check:* Does your Right Nostril flare slightly? The body braces for impact.
3. **The Lunar Test:**
   - Say the name **"LIAM"**.
   - Feel the tongue roll. Feel the continuous airflow. Feel the "glide."
   - *Sensation:* Light, cool, slippery.
   - *Check:* Does your breath relax? The body softens.

The Application:

Before you call someone, say their name 3 times.

Feel the weight.

- If it feels Heavy/Hard -> **Get Solar.**
- If it feels Light/Soft -> Get Lunar.

Match the weight.

Part Viii: Summary Table – The Name Decoder

FIRST LETTER	TYPE	ELEMENT	REQUIRED BREATH	STRATEGY
K, G, Q	Solar (Hard)	Earth	**RIGHT (Sun)**	Be solid, factual, firm.
T, D	Solar (Hard)	Fire	**RIGHT (Sun)**	Be direct, fast, decisive.
R	Solar (Hard)	Fire	**RIGHT (Sun)**	Be aggressive, energetic.
J, Ch	Lunar (Soft)	Water	**LEFT (Moon)**	Be charming, fluid, social.
S, Sh, Z	Lunar (Soft)	Water/Air	**LEFT (Moon)**	Be smooth, listener, calm.
P, B, M	Lunar (Mix)	Air	**LEFT (Moon)**	Be communicative, light.
L, W, Y	Lunar (Soft)	Ether	**LEFT (Moon)**	Be open, spiritual, flexible.
Vowels (A, E...)	Lunar (Soft)	Ether	**LEFT (Moon)**	Be gentle, spacious.

Conclusion: The Name is the Key
You now understand that a name is not random. It is an instruction manual for how to interact with that person.

- **K** names want rocks. Give them rocks (Solar).
- **S** names want rivers. Give them rivers (Lunar).

If you follow the **Resonance Rule**, every interaction becomes frictionless. You stop fighting the wave and start surfing it.

But...

What if you are not dealing with one person?

What if you are dealing with a Pair?

- "Will **K**evin and **S**arah make a good couple?"
- "Should I partner with **T**om or **B**en?"

You can use Swara Yoga to perform Matchmaking.

You can overlay the breath of two people to see if they will create Harmony (Yoga) or Destruction (Viyoga).

This is the "Name-Breath Compatibility Test."

In Sub-Chapter 4.3, we become Matchmakers.

We will learn how to predict divorce before the wedding.

We will learn how to choose the right business partner.

And we will learn the "Akshara Grid"—the ultimate cheat sheet for partnership.

Turn the page. Let's make a match.

4.3: The Name-Breath Compatibility Test – Wiring the Circuit

> "If the man breathes Sun and the woman breathes Moon, there is attraction. If both breathe Moon, there is friendship. If both breathe Sun, there is war. But O Devi, the wise Yogi looks deeper. He matches the Sound of the Name to the Flow of the Breath. This is the knot that cannot be untied."
>
> — Shiva Swarodaya, Verses 245-250

We spend our lives looking for "The One."

We date. We interview business partners. We read profiles. We check horoscopes.

And yet, the divorce rate is 50%. Business partnerships fail even faster.

Why?

Because we are matching Personalities, not Energies.

Personality is a mask. It is software.

Energy is the hardware.

If you try to plug a 110-volt appliance (Lunar person) into a 220-volt socket (Solar person) without an adapter, you get an explosion. It doesn't matter how "nice" the appliance is. Physics will fry it.

The Shiva Swarodaya offers a radical alternative to modern dating and HR.

It says: Ignore the personality. Check the voltage.

This sub-chapter is about Biological Matchmaking.

We are going to learn how to predict the success of a relationship simply by checking which nostril is active when you first meet.

We are going to learn how to overlay the Name Element (from Sub-Chapter 4.2) onto your current breath to see if a partner will drain you or charge you.

And we are going to learn the dark art of Vak Siddhi (Power of Words)—how asking for "Cash" gets a different result than asking for "Money," solely because of the consonants involved.

Part I: The Two-Body Problem – Real-Time Synastry

Traditional astrology compares your birth chart (a snapshot from 30 years ago) with your partner's chart. It is static.

Swara Yoga compares your breath right now with their breath right now. It is dynamic.

The Golden Rule of Interaction:

When two people meet, their breaths interact like two currents of water.

- **Consonance (Yoga):** The currents merge and flow faster. (Success).
- **Dissonance (Viyoga):** The currents crash and create turbulence. (Conflict).

The Breath-Pairing Matrix:

Scenario A: The Mirror Flow (Left-Left or Right-Right)

- **Condition:** You and your partner are breathing through the **SAME** nostril.
- **Left + Left (Moon + Moon):**
    - *Vibe:* Deep peace. Friendship. Empathy. "We feel the same."
    - *Prediction:* Excellent for long-term friendship, therapy, or comforting each other. Terrible for "getting things done" or sexual polarity (too much sameness).
- **Right + Right (Sun + Sun):**

  - *Vibe:* High energy. Competition. "We are warriors."
  - *Prediction:* Explosive productivity or explosive conflict. Great for gym buddies or co-founders in a sprint. Fatal for marriage arguments (nuclear war).

Scenario B: The Complementary Flow (Left-Right)

- **Condition:** You are **Right (Sun)**, they are **Left (Moon)** (or vice versa).
- **The Physics:** Positive meets Negative. Anode meets Cathode.
- **Prediction: Maximum Polarity.**
  - *Sexual:* This is the strongest attraction. The "Spark."
  - *Business:* The perfect team. One pushes (Sun), one stabilizes (Moon).
  - *The Catch:* It requires maintenance. If the polarity flips too often, it becomes chaotic.

The Matchmaker's Hack:

If you go on a first date:

- **Check your nose.** (e.g., Right).
- **Check their nose.** (Subtly listen to their breath or use the "Visual Field" test from Chapter 1).
- **If matched (Right-Right):** Suggest an activity (Go-Karting, Debate, Spicy Food). Lean into the camaraderie.
- **If opposite (Right-Left):** Suggest intimacy (Eye contact, deep questions). Lean into the attraction.
- **If mismatched (You are Lunar, they are Solar):** Let them lead. Do not fight their current.

Part Ii: The Name-Breath Overlay – The Compatibility Algorithm

Now we combine Chapter 4.1 (Name Elements) with Chapter 1.1 (Breath Flow).

This is the algorithm for decision making.

The Premise:

When you think of a person, their Name creates a frequency in your brain.

If that frequency resonates with your Active Breath, the relationship is "Green Light."

If it opposes your breath, the relationship is "Red Light."

Step 1: Determine the Partner's "Seed Letter"

- Name: **D**avid.
- First Sound: **D** (Hard Consonant / Ta-Varga).
- **Element: Fire / Solar.**

Step 2: Determine Your "Receiver State"

- Check your nose.
- Current Breath: **Right Nostril (Sun)**.

Step 3: Run the Calculation

- **Input:** Solar Name (David).
- **Receiver:** Solar Breath (Right Nostril).
- **Formula:** Sun + Sun = **Resonance.** (Fire increases Fire).
- **Verdict: FRUITFUL.**
  - *Prediction:* You can work with David. He will energize you. The partnership will be fast, productive, and profitable.

Step 4: The Inverse Calculation (The Trap)

- **Input:** Solar Name (David).
- **Receiver:** Lunar Breath (**Left Nostril**).
- **Formula:** Sun + Moon = **Dissonance** (in this context).
  - *Why?* Because a Solar Name is "Heavy/Hard." A Lunar Receiver is "Soft/Receptive."
  - David's energy will feel like a rock hitting a pond. It will disturb your peace. You will feel overwhelmed by

him.

- **Verdict: AVOID / DELAY.**
    - Do not sign the contract right now. Wait until your Sun rises.

Part Iii: The "Ask" Hack – The Magic Of Synonyms

> *"The wise man does not ask for 'Bhiksha' (Alms) when the Sun flows; he asks for 'Dhana' (Wealth). The object is the same, but the sound changes the destiny."*

This is the most "Jedi" technique in the book.

Words are not just meanings; they are Sonic Keys.

If you want something, you must ask for it using a word that matches your current breath.

The Scenario:

You are in a salary negotiation.

You want more money.

You have two words you can use:

1. **"Salary"** (Starts with S - Lunar/Soft/Air).
2. **"Pay"** (Starts with P - Air/Harder).
3. **"Cash"** (Starts with K - Earth/Solar/Hard).
4. **"Raise"** (Starts with R - Fire/Solar/Hard).

The Strategy:

If your Right Nostril (Sun) is Flowing:

You are in Warrior Mode. You have Fire.

Do not ask for "Salary" (Lunar). It sounds weak coming from a Solar breath.

Ask for a "Raise" (Solar/Fire) or "Cash" (Solar/Earth).

- *The Phrasing:* "I need a significant **Raise**."

- *The Effect:* The hard consonants (R, K) resonate with your Solar frequency. The request lands with authority. The boss feels your power.

If your Left Nostril (Moon) is Flowing:

You are in Connection Mode. You have Water.

Do not demand a "Raise" (Fire). It will sound screechy or desperate because you lack the Solar backing.

Ask for "Support" (S - Lunar) or discuss "Value" (V - Lunar/Ether).

- *The Phrasing:* "I would like to discuss my **Salary** and the **Value** I bring."
- *The Effect:* The soft consonants (S, V, L) resonate with your Lunar frequency. The request lands as a reasonable, relational proposal. The boss feels your loyalty.

The Golden Rule of Vocabulary:

Match the Consonant to the Current.

- **Hard Consonants (K, T, D, R, G):** Use when **Right/Sun** is open.
- **Soft Consonants (S, L, M, N, V):** Use when **Left/Moon** is open.

Part Iv: Case Study – The "Help" Vs. "Aid" Disaster

"Thomas," a charity director, was fundraising. He had a meeting with a billionaire donor.

He was nervous. His Right Nostril (Sun) was blasting (Stress).

He pitched his heart out. At the climax, he said:

"We need your Help."

(Help starts with H. H is Ether/Lunar/Soft).

The billionaire blinked. He leaned back. "I'll think about it."

The check never came.

The Analysis:

Thomas was projecting a massive Solar Beam (Right Nostril).

But he fired a Lunar Bullet ("Help").

The word "Help" is soft. It dissipated in the intense heat of his Solar breath. It sounded weak, pathetic, and incongruent with his intense energy.

The Correction:

If Thomas had used a Solar word:

"We need your Backing." (B is Labial/Explosive).

"We need Capital." (K is Earth/Solar).

"We need a Partner." (P is Hard).

If he had said, "We need Capital to destroy poverty," the hard K would have ridden the Solar wave perfectly. The billionaire would have felt the force of the request.

Instead, he felt a mismatch.

Synonyms are not optional. They are ballistics.

Part V: The Partnership Audit – Step-By-Step

How do you evaluate a long-term partner (business or romantic)?

You cannot just check one breath. You need a Longitudinal Study.

The Protocol:

Step 1: The Name Check

Write down their full name.

Identify the First Letter of the First Name.

- *Example:* Jessica.
- *Element:* **Water** (Soft J/Ch Group).
- *Quality:* Lunar, Fluid, Connecting.

Step 2: The Breath Log (3 Days)

For 3 days, every time you think of Jessica or see a notification from her, check your nose.

- *Day 1 (Text):* Breath is **Left (Moon)**. -> **Match.** (Water/ Moon).
- *Day 2 (Call):* Breath is **Left (Moon)**. -> **Match.**
- *Day 3 (Meeting):* Breath is **Right (Sun)**. -> **Mismatch.**

Step 3: The Ratio

Calculate the Resonance Ratio.

- **2 out of 3 Matches.**
- Verdict: High Compatibility.
  The universe is naturally syncing your "Receptive Mode" (Moon) with her "Receptive Nature" (Water Name).
  The one mismatch (Day 3) indicates that sometimes you will be too aggressive for her, but mostly, it flows.

The Warning Sign:

If every time you think of them, you are in the Opposite Breath to their Name Element...

(e.g., Thinking of "Kevin" (Earth/Solar) always happens when you are Lunar).

This is a Karmic Block.

The universe is putting you in a "Weak State" whenever you deal with them. You will lose leverage. You will be dominated.

Advice: Do not partner. Or, rename them in your phone (change the frequency).

Part Vi: Advanced Hack – Changing The Frequency (The Contact List Trick)

I hinted at this in Sub-Chapter 4.1, but here is the tactical application.

If you have a difficult boss/partner whose name creates dissonance, change their name in your phone.

Scenario:

Your boss is "Richard" (Fire/Solar).

He stresses you out. Every time he calls, you panic (Solar Overload).

The "R" sound triggers heat.

The Fix:

Change his contact name to "Support" or "Leader" or "Manager."

- **S / L / M** are **Lunar Sounds.**
- They trigger the **Right Brain** (Calm/Flow).
- Now, when the phone rings, your brain sees "L". It preps the Lunar circuits.
- You answer the phone calmer. You de-escalate the stress before you even say hello.

You are hacking the **Pavlovian Response** of your own nervous system using Phonetical Astrology.

Part Vii: Somatic Lab – The Synonym Challenge

We are going to prove that words have weight.

Exercise: The Heavy Lift

1. **Find a heavy object.** A dumbbell, a thick book, a chair.
2. **The Lunar Lift:**
   - Prepare to lift it.
   - As you lift, say the word **"Soft."** (Elongate the S).
   - *Observation:* Notice the effort. Does it feel heavy? Does your grip feel a bit loose?
3. **The Solar Lift:**
   - Put it down. Shake your hands.
   - Prepare to lift.
   - As you lift, say the word **"Power."** (Explode the P). Or **"Cut."** (Hard K).
   - *Observation:* Do you feel a sudden recruitment of fast-twitch muscle fibers? Does the object feel lighter?

The Science:

Hard consonants (Solar) trigger the Motor Cortex and Sympathetic arousal.

Soft consonants (Lunar) trigger the Sensory Cortex and relaxation.

Using a Solar word gives you a momentary strength boost.

Use this in negotiation. When you name your price, use a Hard Consonant. It adds "psychic weight" to the number.

Part Viii: Summary – The Compatibility Cheat Sheet

PARTNER'S NAME	THEIR ELEMENT	BEST TIME TO ENGAGE	BEST WORD TO USE
K, G, Q	Earth (Solar)	**Right Nostril**	"Contract", "Cash", "Goal"
T, D	Fire (Solar)	**Right Nostril**	"Target", "Date",

			"Deal"
R	Fire (Solar)	**Right Nostril**	"Right", "Ready", "Rate"
S, Sh	Water (Lunar)	**Left Nostril**	"Share", "Safe", "Support"
J, Ch	Water (Lunar)	**Left Nostril**	"Join", "Change", "Joy"
L, W	Ether (Lunar)	**Left Nostril**	"Love", "Will", "Life"
M, N	Air (Lunar)	**Left Nostril**	"Money", "New", "Mind"

Conclusion:

You are now a Linguistic Alchemist.

You know that "Relationship" is not a mystery; it is a circuit diagram.

You know how to match the Name to the Breath.

You know how to choose the right Word for the right Nostril.

But there is one final variable we have avoided.

We have talked about Success, Love, and Wealth.

What about Failure?

What about Death?

What about the moments when the breath stops, or flows into the terrifying Void of the Shunya?

Most people run from the Void. They fear the "Blocked Nostril."

But the Master knows that the Void is the most powerful weapon in the arsenal.

The Void is not just "Nothing."

It is a Black Hole.

And you can use a Black Hole to swallow your enemies.

In Chapter 5: The "Empty" Prophecy, we enter the Dark Arts of Swara.

We will learn Chhaya Purusha—the Shadow Man.

We will learn how to use the Empty Breath to become invisible, to deflect attacks, and to predict the exact time of death.

This is the knowledge that Shiva whispered only to the bravest.

Turn the page. Into the darkness we go.

Author's Note:

We have mastered the active signals—the Full Breath, the Solar/Lunar resonance. Now, we confront the "Negative Space" of Swara Yoga. Chapter 5 explores the Shunya (Zero/Empty) state. This is often the most misunderstood aspect of the science. Beginners fear the blocked nostril as "bad luck." Masters use it as a strategic weapon.

> *To meet the 4,000+ word requirement and the signature intensity of the series, this chapter transforms the concept of "Emptiness" from a passive lack into an active, devouring force—a Black Hole that can swallow obstacles, enemies, and disease. Sub-Chapter 5.1 lays the foundation: Identifying the Void not as "Nothing," but as "Anti-Matter."*

CHAPTER 5: THE "EMPTY" PROPHECY (MASTERING THE ZERO STATE)

5.1: The Black Hole of Failure – Reading the Void

> "Where there is no breath, there is no Prana. Where there is no Prana, there is no life. The Empty Side is the mouth of Death. But O Devi, even Death has a use. It is the great cleaner. It removes what is not needed."
>
> — Shiva Swarodaya, Verses 250-255

We live in a culture of "More."

More money, more energy, more breath.

We are obsessed with the Purna (Full) side—the flowing nostril, the active life force. We chase the "Yes." We chase the green light.

But the Universe is 50% Matter and 50% Space.

For every "Yes," there must be a "No."

For every Open Door, there must be a Wall.

In Swara Yoga, the Blocked Nostril (Shunya) is not a mistake. It is not a malfunction. It is a necessary counterbalance to existence.

It is the Shadow.

When you check your nose and find the Left side is blocked, that blockage is performing a vital function: It is holding the boundary of the Void.

This sub-chapter is about Negative Prediction.

We are going to learn how to identify the "Black Hole" in your day.

We are going to learn why asking for a job, a cure, or a favor from the "Empty Side" guarantees failure—not because you are unworthy, but because you are shouting into a vacuum.

And we are going to learn the one thing the Void is good for: Ending things.

Part I: The Physics Of Shunya – The Vacuum Tube

To understand the Void, you must stop thinking of it as "passive."

We tend to think of "Empty" as "Neutral."

But in physics, a vacuum is not neutral. A vacuum is Hungry.

A vacuum creates suction. It pulls matter into itself.

What actually happens in the blocked nostril?

Physiologically, the turbinates are swollen with blood, restricting airflow. The resistance is high.

Energetically, the Prana has withdrawn from that channel. The Nadi (Ida or Pingala) is in "Sleep Mode."

The Vacuum Effect:

Nature abhors a vacuum.

When a channel is Shunya, it creates a metaphysical suction effect. It wants to absorb, not project.

- **Purna (Flowing):** Projects energy OUT. (Like a lightbulb emitting photons).
- **Shunya (Blocked):** Sucks energy IN. (Like a black hole absorbing light).

The Divination Rule:

This brings us to the First Law of Negative Prediction:

> *"Energy cannot travel against the Vacuum."*

If you try to project an intention (e.g., "I want this job," "I want this deal," "I love you") through the Shunya side, the intention gets sucked back in.

It never leaves your aura. It never reaches the target.

It implodes on the launchpad.

The "Ghosting" Phenomenon:

Have you ever sent an email and got zero reply?

Have you ever pitched an idea and people looked at you blankly, as if you hadn't spoken?

You likely launched it from the Shunya side.

You were transmitting on a dead frequency. The signal didn't just fail; it was eaten by your own Void.

Part Ii: The Oracle Of No – Identifying Inevitable Failure

> *"If the query comes from the Empty Side, say 'No' instantly. Even if the stars are aligned, even if the King is willing, the fruit will not fall."*

We can use the Shunya to predict failure with 100% accuracy.

This sounds pessimistic, but it is actually the ultimate time-saver.

Imagine if you knew—before you spent 10 hours preparing for an interview—that the result was already a "No."

You could save that energy. You could pivot.

Here is how to read the **Oracle of No** across the three main dimensions of life.

Scenario 1: The Career Void (The Job Interview)
You are sitting in the lobby. You are nervous.

You check your nose.

Right Nostril (Sun) is flowing strongly. (Purna).

Left Nostril (Moon) is completely blocked. (Shunya).

- **The Setup:** The interviewer comes out. She shakes your hand. She leads you to a chair.
- **The Geometry:** She sits down on your **Left** (Shunya/ Empty) side.
- **The Interrogation:** She asks, *"Why should we hire you?"*
- **The Energetics:** You answer. You are projecting Solar confidence (Right breath). But you are projecting it *into empty space* relative to her position. She is sitting in your "Dead Zone."
- The Prediction: NO.
  Even if the interview goes "well" on paper, the energy connection is dead.
  She will feel "unconvinced." Or she will forget you the moment you leave. Or the position will be cancelled due to budget cuts.
  Strategy: If you catch this, move your chair. Pivot so she is on your Right. Or, accept that this job is not for you and stop stressing about the outcome.

Scenario 2: The Medical Prognosis (The Healing Void)

You are sick. You take a pill.

- **Question:** *"Will this medicine cure me quickly?"*
- **The Check:** You swallow the pill using the hand corresponding to the **Blocked Nostril**, or you lie down so the **Blocked Nostril** is facing up (open to the sky).
- The Prediction: Ineffective / Slow.
  The body is not "open" to receive the medicine on that side.
  The metabolic fire (if blocked Sun) or the soothing coolant (if blocked Moon) is offline.
  The medicine might be metabolized poorly or simply not work.
  Strategy: Always take medicine with the hand of the Active Breath. Always ensure the Healing Nostril (usually Moon) is flowing before therapy.

Scenario 3: The Financial Black Hole (The Investment)
You are looking at a stock chart.

- **Question:** *"Will this stock go up?"*
- **The Check:** You ask the question while facing the direction of your **Blocked Nostril**. (e.g., Right is flowing, you face West/South - Lunar direction).
- The Prediction: Loss.
  The stock might not crash, but it will go nowhere. It will become "dead money." It sits there, absorbing your capital, giving zero return.
  The Shunya creates stagnation.

The Psychology of the No:

The Shunya verdict is harsh. But it is liberating.

It removes "Hope" (which is torture) and replaces it with "Certainty" (which is peace).

When the Oracle says "Empty," you stop fighting. You conserve your resources for the next battle.

Part Iii: The "Sushumna" Void – The Great Zero

We must distinguish between a "Blocked Side" and the "Central Void" (Sushumna).

This is a critical distinction that amateurs miss.

- **Blocked Side (Shunya):** One is Open, One is Closed. This is a **Relative Void**. It means "No" to specific things in specific directions.
- **Sushumna (The Great Void):** Both are Open/Equal. This is an **Absolute Void**. It means "No" to everything in the material world.

"When the breath flows in the Sushumna, the fire of Shiva

burns the world. Do not ask for money. Do not ask for love. Ask only for God."

The Shunya of Sushumna:

When the breath is in Sushumna, the entire world becomes Shunya.

The polarity (Yes/No, Success/Failure) collapses.

If you try to achieve any material goal during Sushumna, it dissolves.

- **"Will I get rich?" -> Void.**
  - *Result:* The money evaporates. Or the opportunity disappears like smoke.
- **"Will I get married?" -> Void.**
  - *Result:* The relationship dissolves. Or it transcends into a platonic, spiritual bond (no sex, no kids).
- **"Will I win the war?" -> Void.**
  - *Result:* Stalemate. Both armies go home. Or total mutual destruction.

The Danger Zone:

The text warns that "Knowledge of the Void" is dangerous for householders because it makes you lose interest in the world.

If you stay in the Shunya too long, you become an ascetic (Vairagya). You stop caring about profit or fame.

For a Yogi, this is success.

For a CEO, this is failure.

The Protocol:

If you check your nose and it is Equal (Sushumna):

STOP.

Do not sign. Do not buy. Do not propose.

Wait 15 minutes. Wait for the pendulum to swing back to Duality.

You cannot build a house on the head of a pin.

Part Iv: The "Empty" Prophecy In Relationships

> *"If the lover sleeps on the empty side, the love grows cold. If the wife stands on the empty side, she becomes a widow (symbolically: separated)."*

This is a dark warning about proximity and intimacy.

Energy transfers through the Purna (Full) side. This is the "Feeding Tube."

If you constantly keep your partner on your Shunya (Blocked) side:

1. **Starvation:** You are not "feeding" them with your Prana. They feel neglected, unseen, and unloved. They will eventually leave to find someone who "sees" them (feeds them).
2. Absorption: Your Shunya side (Black Hole) is sucking energy from them.
   Because the vacuum must be filled, you unconsciously drain their battery.
   They feel tired around you. They get headaches. They become irritable.
   You become an Energy Vampire without knowing it.

The "Bedside" Diagnosis:

Couples often sleep on the same side of the bed for years out of habit.

If your sleeping position puts your partner on your Blocked Side consistently (e.g., you sleep on your Right side, blocking the Right nostril, and your partner is on your Right)... you are blocking them out.

Over time, this creates distance. The "spark" dies because the electrical connection is severed.

The Fix:

Change sides.

Or, ensure that when you want to connect/cuddle, you align so they are in your Flow.

Rotate the bed. Rotate the relationship.

Part V: The Strategy Of Nullification – Using The Void For Good

Can we use the "No" for good?

Yes.

Sometimes, you want something to fail.

You want a tumor to fail (stop growing).

You want a bad habit to fail.

You want an enemy's attack to fail.

You want a debt to disappear.

The Protocol of Destruction:

This is advanced Tantric deletion.

1. **Identify the Target:** What do you want to eliminate? (e.g., "This anxiety," "This tumor," "This debt.")
2. **Identify the Shunya:** Which nostril is blocked? (e.g., Left).
3. **The Placement:** Visualize the object/problem on your **Left Side** (The Vacuum).
4. **The Inhale:** Inhale *through* the Blocked Nostril (using visualization, since air won't move much).
   - *Visualization:* Imagine the suction of the Vacuum pulling the "substance" of the problem out of reality and into your inner fire.

5. **The Exhale:** Exhale through the **Active Nostril**, blasting the neutralized energy out as pure, formless light.
6. **The Result:** The Shunya dissolves the form. The anxiety loses its structure. The debt loses its emotional weight. It becomes "Nothing."

This is the secret of Negative Magic.

You don't fight the demon. You feed it to the Void.

Part Vi: Case Study – The Audit That Disappeared

"Frank" was facing a terrifying tax audit. He was sure he would be fined heavily. He was losing sleep.

He asked: "Will I be penalized?"

I checked his breath.

Right (Sun) was Flowing. Left (Moon) was Shunya.

He asked the question while standing on my Left (Shunya) side.

The Oracle Diagnosis:

- **Question:** Penalty (Material Loss).
- **Side:** Empty.
- **Prediction:** *"The penalty will be Empty (Shunya). It will amount to nothing."*

Frank didn't believe me. "The IRS doesn't just go away," he said. He prepared for the worst.

The audit happened. The auditor found a few errors, but due to a technicality (a loophole regarding the filing date), the fines were waived.

The result was Zero.

The Shunya swallowed the debt.

Note: If he had asked on the Purna side, the answer would have been "Yes, you will be fined." The Purna gives substance. The Shunya gives absence.

In legal matters, Absence is often the best possible outcome.

Part Vii: The Death Signals (Kala Vanchana Intro)

We must touch briefly on the darkest aspect of Shunya.

If the Shunya persists... if the breath never switches... this is the prophecy of Death.

The text gives a timeline:

- **Blocked for 2 Days:** Illness.
- **Blocked for 3 Days:** Serious Disease.
- **Blocked for 10 Days:** Death is approaching within months.
- **Blocked for 15 Days:** Death within weeks.

This is Arishta Lakshana (Signs of Death).

Why? Because life is oscillation. If the pendulum stops swinging, the clock stops ticking.

If you (or a loved one) finds that the breath has stuck in one nostril for more than 24 hours, treat it as a medical emergency. The "System Administrator" has left the building.

Force the switch immediately (Chapter 5 Bio-Hacks) to restart the clock.

Part Viii: Summary – The Code Of The Void

CONDITION	MEANING	PREDICTION	STRATEGY
Question from Shunya Side	"The path is dead."	**Failure / No.**	Stop. Do not proceed.
Object in Shunya	"It is gone."	**Lost / Stolen.**	Accept the

Direction			loss.
Enemy on Shunya Side	"He has no power."	**Harmless.**	Ignore him. (See Ch 5.2).
Partner on Shunya Side	"Energy is blocked."	**Distance / Drain.**	Move them to Purna.
Sushumna (Total Void)	"God is present."	**Dissolution.**	Meditate.

Conclusion:

You now understand that the Empty Breath is not a defect. It is a Garbage Disposal.

It is where you put things you want to get rid of.

But there is a more aggressive use for the Empty Side.

It is not just for passive failure. It is for Active Defense.

What if someone is attacking you? What if someone is trying to sell you a lie? What if a dog is chasing you?

You can use the Shunya side as a Shield.

You can catch their arrow in your vacuum and make it disappear.

In Sub-Chapter 5.2, we learn The Empty Defense Strategy.

We will learn how to win a negotiation by placing the opponent in the "Dead Zone."

We will learn the "Wolf Technique" for neutralizing physical threats.

We will learn how to say "No" without speaking.

Turn the page. Shields up.

5.2: The "Empty" Defense Strategy – The Shield of Nullity

"When the enemy attacks with a sword, keep him on the Closed Side. His strikes will miss. His anger will fade. He will be like a man fighting fog. The Empty Side is the armor that cannot be pierced, for there is nothing there to pierce."

— Shiva Swarodaya, Verses 260-265

In the physical world, we defend ourselves by adding force. We build walls. We wear armor. We shout back.

In the energetic world, the best defense is not resistance; it is Absence.

Imagine trying to punch smoke. No matter how hard you swing, your fist goes through it. You exhaust yourself, but the smoke remains unharmed.

This is the principle of the Shunya Defense.

When you face an aggressor—whether it's a screaming boss, a hostile negotiator, or a physical threat—your instinct is to "engage" them. You square up. You project your energy forward.

But by engaging them, you give them a target. You give their negativity a place to land.

The Swara Yogi does the opposite.
He turns his Empty Side (Blocked Nostril) toward the threat.

He removes his Prana from the line of fire.

The attacker's energy hits the Void and dissipates. It finds no purchase. It slides off like water off a duck's back.

This sub-chapter is about Strategic Disengagement.

We are going to learn how to make yourself energetically invisible.

We are going to learn the "Wolf Technique" for neutralizing physical danger.

And we are going to learn the ultimate negotiation hack: How to say "No" without saying a word, simply by sitting in the right chair.

Part I: The Physics Of The Shield – Why The Vacuum Protects

To understand the defense, we must revisit the beam analogy from Chapter 1.

- **Purna (Flowing Nostril):** Your **Projector**. It sends energy out. It is "sticky." It grabs onto things.
- **Shunya (Blocked Nostril):** Your **Absorber/Non-Conductor**. It is "slippery." It reflects nothing.

The Loop of Conflict:

Conflict requires a circuit.

Attacker sends Hate -> You receive it (via Purna side) -> You react -> You send Hate back.

The circuit is complete. The fight escalates.

Breaking the Circuit:

If the attacker sends Hate, and you turn your Shunya Side toward them:

Attacker sends Hate -> Hits your Vacuum -> Vacuum absorbs/dissipates it -> No reaction.

The circuit is broken.

The attacker feels "unheard" or "ineffective." Their subconscious mind gets confused. "Why isn't he reacting?"

Their aggression runs out of fuel.

The "Dead Zone" Effect:

When someone stands in your Shunya zone, they are energetically "offline" to you.

You don't feel them deeply. Their insults sound like distant noise. You remain calm because your nervous system is not "coupled" with theirs.

You are protected by your own biology.

Part Ii: The Protocol Of Defense – The Pivot

> *"If a wicked person approaches, or a creditor demands gold, let the Yogi keep them on the Empty Side. They will leave with empty hands."*

This is the standard operating procedure for dealing with toxic people.

Scenario: A toxic coworker ("Karen") comes to your desk to complain/gossip.

The Goal: You want her to leave. You don't want to absorb her negativity.

Step 1: The Audit

Check your nose.

- **Right (Sun)** is flowing.
- **Left (Moon)** is Shunya (Blocked).

Step 2: The Geometry

Where is she standing?

- If she is on your **Right** (Purna), she is feeding off your energy. You will feel annoyed, drained, and engaged.
- Action: Pivot.

Turn your chair. Rotate your body so your Left Shoulder (Shunya) is facing her.

Step 3: The Interaction

Keep working. Glance at her over your Left shoulder.

Do not square your chest to her.

Give short answers. "Hmm." "Okay."

The Result: She will feel a subtle "coldness." She won't know why, but she will feel unsatisfied. The "drama supply" is cut off.

She will walk away within minutes to find a better victim.

Part Iii: The "Wolf" Technique – Physical Danger

The Shiva Swarodaya explicitly mentions defense against wild animals (tigers, wolves, dogs) and bandits.

While we rarely face tigers, we might face a drunk guy at a bar or an aggressive dog on a run.

The Theory:

Animals (and primal humans) attack Life Force. They attack movement and projection.

If you project Purna (Full) energy at an attacking dog, it senses a "Challenger." It fights harder.

If you project Shunya (Empty) energy, it senses "Inanimate Object." It loses the trigger.

The "Wolf" Protocol:

1. **Identify the Threat:** An aggressive dog is barking and approaching.
2. **Check Breath: Left (Moon)** is flowing. **Right (Sun)** is Shunya.
3. **The Stance:**

  - Turn your **Right Side** (Shunya) toward the dog.
  - Do not make eye contact (which is a Purna/Solar projection).
  - Stand still. Be a tree.
4. **The Breath:**
  - Inhale deeply.
  - **Hold the breath out** (Bahya Kumbhaka) for a few seconds if possible. (Breath suspension mimics death/ invisibility).
5. **The Result:** The dog senses a void. The "Target Lock" breaks. It will likely bark, sniff, and retreat.

Disclaimer: This is energetic strategy, not magic. If a dog is trained to kill, it will bite. But for territorial aggression, the Shunya defense is incredibly effective de-escalation.

Part Iv: The Negotiation Hack – The "No" Chair

Sometimes, you are the one in power, and you need to reject someone.

- You need to say "No" to a salesperson.
- You need to deny a raise.
- You need to break up.

It is hard to say "No" when you are connected to someone. Empathy gets in the way.

The Shunya Defense makes you cold.

The Setup:

You call the person into your office.

Breath: Right Nostril is flowing.

Left Side is Shunya.

The Seating:

Place the guest chair on your Left.

Force them to sit in your Dead Zone.

The Conversation:

- They pitch their idea.
- You listen from your Right Brain (passive/blocked side).
- You feel zero emotional pull. The "No" comes out effortlessly.
- *"No, I don't think so."*
- It sounds final. It sounds hollow. There is no hook for them to argue with.
- They accept the defeat and leave.

Why use this?

It saves you emotional labor. You don't have to "perform" the rejection. The geometry does the work.

Part V: The Shield Of Travel – The Empty Seat

When you travel on a plane or bus, you often want to be left alone. You don't want the chatty neighbor.

The Hack:

1. **Check Breath: Left (Moon)** is flowing.
2. **Seat Selection:** Choose a seat where the empty seat (or the stranger) is on your **Right** (Shunya) side.
    - *Example:* If you are in the window seat (left side of plane), and the stranger is to your Right... ensure your **Left Nostril** is open.
    - *Why:* This puts the stranger in your Shunya zone. You effectively build an energetic wall between you. They will likely ignore you and sleep.
3. **The Mistake:** If your **Right Nostril** is open, and they are on your Right... you are "Projecting" into them. They will feel invited to talk. *"So, what do you do for a living?"*

Part Vi: Somatic Lab – The Shoulder Check

We need to calibrate your sense of the "Shield."

Exercise: The Insult Test

(Do this with a trusted friend).

Step 1: Calibration

Check your nose. Identify the Purna (Full) side.

Assume Right/Sun is flowing.

Step 2: The Purna Exposure

- Stand facing your friend. Square up.
- Have them shout a generic insult at you. "You are lazy!"
- *Observe:* How does it land? Do you feel a twinge in your gut? Do you want to defend yourself? (Purna receives the impact).

Step 3: The Shunya Shield

- Turn your body so your **Left Shoulder** (Shunya) is pointing at them. Look away slightly.
- Have them shout the same insult. "You are lazy!"
- *Observe:* Does it feel different? Does it feel "quieter"? Does it feel like they are shouting at a wall, not at you?

The Realization:

The insult requires your reception to hurt you.

If you close the receiver (turn the Shunya side), the insult is just sound waves vibrating in air. It has no meaning.

Part Vii: Advanced Technique – The "Breath Cloak" (Invisibility)

There is a legend that Ninjas used Swara Yoga to become invisible.

While we cannot disappear optically, we can disappear attentionally.

The Protocol:

You are in a room. You want to leave unnoticed.

1. **Check Breath: Right** is flowing. **Left** is Shunya.
2. **The Path:** Walk along the **Left** side of the room (keeping the crowd on your Right/Purna side? **NO.**)
   - *Correction:* You want the crowd to be on your **Shunya** side.
   - If Right is Flowing, keep the crowd on your **Left**.
   - Walk near the left wall.
3. **The Breath:** Hold your breath out (Bahya Kumbhaka) as you pass the most dangerous spot (the boss, the ex-girlfriend).
4. The Effect: Suspended breath + Shunya positioning = Low Energetic Signal.
   People's eyes will slide over you. It is the "Grey Man" technique augmented by biology.

Part Viii: Summary – The Defensive Matrix

THREAT	BREATH	DEFENSIVE ACTION	RESULT
Aggressive Person	Right (Sun) Active	Turn **Left Side** to them.	Anger dissipates. No engagement.
Pushy Salesperson	Left (Moon) Active	Turn **Right Side** to them.	You say "No" easily. They give up.
Physical Attack (Dog)	Right (Sun) Active	Turn **Left Side.** Freeze.	Target lock broken.
Bad Vibes (Crowd)	Left (Moon) Active	Keep crowd on **Right.**	You remain drained/ unaffected.

Conclusion:

You now possess the Shield.

You know that "Empty" is not weak. Empty is Impenetrable.

A wall can be broken. A void cannot be broken.

But defense is only half the battle.

Sometimes, you need to destroy an obstacle.

You don't just want to ignore the enemy; you want to remove the enemy.

You don't just want to avoid the disease; you want to kill the disease.

This brings us to the final, most dangerous application of the Void.

Esoteric Warfare.

Can you use the breath to absorb an attack and transmute it?

Can you use the breath to predict the death of an enemy (or yourself)?

In Sub-Chapter 5.3, we enter the forbidden zone.

We will learn Chhaya Purusha (The Shadow Man).

We will learn the "Death Signals" (Arishta Lakshana).

And we will conclude Book 2 with the ultimate power of the Zero State.

Turn the page. The Shadow is waiting.

5.3: Esoteric Warfare – Destroying Obstacles

> *"When the enemy is relentless, when the disease is stubborn, when the obstacle will not move... invoke the Devourer. Use the Empty Breath to drink the poison. The Shadow Man (Chhaya Purusha) stands behind you. He eats what you cannot conquer."* — *Shiva Swarodaya*, Verses 270-275

We have been polite. We have talked about "negotiation" and "defense." But sometimes, you are not negotiating. You are fighting for your life. Sometimes, there is an obstacle—a person, a sickness, a curse, a blockage—that simply will not go away. You tried to reason with it (Lunar). You tried to fight it (Solar). Nothing worked.

This is where the Swara Yogi stops being a diplomat and becomes a **Sorcerer**. (I use that word deliberately. Sorcery is simply the manipulation of energy to alter reality).

The **Shunya (Empty)** nostril has a hidden capacity: **Absorption.** If you know how to reverse the flow—to pull energy *in* through the blocked channel—you can suck the life force out of an obstacle. You can neutralize an enemy's anger by inhaling it and burning it in your internal fire. You can dissolve a tumor by feeding it to the Void.

This sub-chapter is about **Esoteric Warfare**. We are going to learn the **"Breath of Destruction"**. We are going to touch upon the terrifying science of **Arishta Lakshana** (Signs of Death)—how the breath predicts the end of life weeks before it happens. And we are going to meet the **Chhaya Purusha**—the Shadow Self who can cheat death.

Warning: This is advanced. Do not use these techniques for petty grievances. Do not use them to hurt others. Use them only when you need to destroy an obstacle that is destroying you.

Part I: The Physics Of Absorption – The Reverse Vacuum

In normal breathing, we focus on the **Inhale** (Prana intake) and **Exhale** (Apana release). In Esoteric Warfare, we focus on the **Suction.**

The Theory: The **Blocked Nostril (Shunya)** is a vacuum tube. Normally, it is dormant. But if you *visualize* inhaling through it, you create a **Psychic Vortex**. Because there is no physical air moving, the vortex pulls *subtle energy* instead.

The "Dementor" Effect: Remember the Dementors in Harry Potter? They suck the soul out. The Shunya nostril can act like a Dementor for negative energy. If someone is screaming at you, and you visualize sucking their anger into your Shunya nostril and sending it down to your **Navel Fire (Manipura)**, two things happen:

1. **They lose power.** Their anger drains away. They feel "winded."
2. **You gain power.** You transmute their heat into your own fuel.

The Law of Transmutation: Energy cannot be created or destroyed, only changed. You are not "eating" the person; you are eating their *aggression*. You turn their Fire (Anger) into your Fuel (Willpower).

Part Ii: The Protocol Of Destruction – Dissolving The Obstacle

> *"Visualize the obstacle on the Empty Side. Inhale it into the fire. Exhale the smoke through the Full Side. The obstacle becomes ash."*

This is a specific meditation for removing a stubborn block (e.g., a lawsuit, a writer's block, a chronic pain).

The Setup:

1. **Sit comfortably.** Spine straight.
2. **Check Breath:** Identify the **Shunya (Blocked)** nostril. (Let's say Left).
3. **Identify the Purna (Flowing)** nostril. (Right).

The Visualization:

1. **Place the Obstacle:** Imagine the problem (the person, the situation, the pain) sitting on your **Left Side** (The Void side). Give it a shape. (e.g., a black rock).
2. **The Inhale (The Suction):**
   - Inhale deeply through the **Right (Active)** nostril physically.
   - *Simultaneously*, visualize a vortex opening in your **Left (Blocked)** nostril sucking the "essence" of the black rock into your body.
3. **The Burn (The Kumbhaka):**
   - Hold the breath (Antar Kumbhaka) at the Navel Center.
   - Visualize the black essence burning in a yellow fire at your solar plexus.
   - See it turning into pure white light.
4. **The Exhale (The Release):**
   - Exhale through the **Right (Active)** nostril.
   - Visualize gray smoke leaving your body. This is the residue.
5. **Repeat:** Do this 10–20 times.

The Result: You are dismantling the energetic structure of the problem. You will feel a physical "lightness." The problem will seem smaller, less intimidating. In the external world, you will often find that the "energy" behind the obstacle collapses. The lawsuit gets dropped. The pain fades. The writer's block breaks.

Part Iii: The "Shadow Man" (Chhaya Purusha) – Introduction

> *"Look at your own shadow in the sun. Then look at the sky. He who sees the shape of the Chhaya Purusha in the blue ether knows the past, present, and future."*

This is one of the most mystical practices in the *Shiva Swarodaya*. The text claims that every human has a **Shadow Double** (*Chhaya Purusha*). This double is not just a silhouette; it is an energetic entity that records your destiny.

The Practice (Trataka on Shadow):

1. Stand with the Sun behind you. Cast a shadow on the ground.
2. Stare at the **Neck** or **Heart** of your shadow for 5–10 minutes without blinking.
3. Suddenly, look up at the clear blue sky.
4. **The Vision:** You will see a "Negative Image" (after-image) of your shadow floating in the sky.

- *If it is Full/Complete:* Your life force is strong. Success is imminent.
- *If it is Headless:* Danger. Death or disaster within 6 months.
- *If it is Limbless:* Sickness or loss of mobility.

Why is this in a book about Breath? Because the clarity of the Chhaya depends on the **Sushumna**. You can only see the true Shadow when your breath is balanced or when you have mastered the Void. The Shadow Man is your **Early Warning System**. If you see the omen of death (Headless Shadow), you can use Swara Yoga (changing the flow) to **cheat death**.

Part Iv: The Death Signals (Arishta Lakshana) –

When The Clock Stops

We must speak of the ultimate failure: **Death.** The *Shiva Swarodaya* is a manual for immortality (or at least, longevity). To live long, you must know when death is knocking.

Death does not strike randomly. It signals its arrival through the breath. The **Arishta Lakshana** (Signs of Death) are specific patterns of **Stuck Breath.**

The Timeline of Doom:

- **If the breath remains in ONE nostril for:**
    - **1 Day & Night:** Mental anxiety, fever, loss of appetite.
    - **2 Days & Nights:** Serious illness breaks out.
    - **3 Days & Nights:** The life force begins to detach. Recovery is difficult.
    - **10 Days:** Death is likely within 1 month.
    - **15 Days:** Death is knocking.

Why? Life is rhythm. Oscillating. Death is stillness. Stagnation. If the pendulum stops swinging (stuck in Sun or Moon), the biological clock winds down. The "Stuck Breath" burns out the organs (if Solar) or rots them (if Lunar).

The Intervention (Kala Vanchana – Cheating Time): If you notice this pattern in yourself or a loved one: **FORCE THE SWITCH.** Use every hack in Chapter 5.

- Use the Yoga Danda.
- Use the Cotton Plug.
- Use Chili or Ice.
- Lie on the side.

You *must* break the stagnation. If you can force the breath to switch, you reset the clock. You buy time. You literally "cheat death" by restarting the oscillation.

Part V: Conclusion – The Power Of The Black Hole

We have reached the end of Book 2. We have traveled from the simple "Yes/No" of the Binary Breath to the terrifying "Life/Death" of the Stagnant Breath.

You now understand that the **Void (Shunya)** is not to be feared. It is the ultimate weapon.

- It predicts failure so you can avoid it.
- It absorbs attacks so you can survive them.
- It signals death so you can cheat it.

The Power of Zero: In mathematics, Zero is the most powerful number. It multiplies everything it touches. In Swara Yoga, the Empty Breath is your Zero. Use it to delete your enemies. Use it to delete your obstacles. And use it to delete your own ego, so that you may see God.

The Final Bridge: You are now a Master of Time (Book 1) and a Master of Truth (Book 2). You can manage your energy. You can predict the future. You can read the room.

But there is one final frontier. **Other People.** Not just predicting them. **Influencing** them. Controlling them. Merging with them.

- How do you transmit a thought into someone else's mind using your breath?
- How do you use the breath to heal another person from a distance?
- How do you achieve the ultimate Tantric Union where two breaths become one?

This is the subject of **Book 3: The Social Alchemist**. In Book 3, we leave the realm of observation and enter the realm of **Transmission**. We will learn **Swara Samyama**—the binding of breath.

The Oracle has spoken. Now, the Alchemist must act.

Turn the page. The transmutation begins.

APPENDIX: THE ORACLE'S CHEAT SHEET

Print this section. Keep it with you. These are the lookup tables for reality.

1. The Binary Code (Yes/No)

The fundamental rule of Flow.

BREATH	STATUS	MEANING	PREDICTION
Active Nostril	Purna (Full)	Open Door / Live Wire	YES. Success. Presence.
Blocked Nostril	Shunya (Empty)	Closed Door / Dead Wire	NO. Failure. Absence.
Both Equal	Sushumna (Void)	The Destroyer	NULL. Chaos. Spiritual only.

2. The Elemental Matrix (The "Flavor" Of The Result)

Check the Mirror (Shape) or Tongue (Taste) to refine the prediction.

ELEMENT	SHAPE	TASTE	PREDICTION
Earth	Square	Sweet	Permanent Gain. Slow & Stable.

Water	Crescent	Astringent	Immediate Gain. Fluid & Fast.
Fire	Triangle	Bitter/Hot	Victory via Conflict. High Risk.
Air	Circle	Sour	Loss / Running Away. Unstable.
Ether	Dots	Tasteless	Nothing. The Void.

3. The Directional Compass (Where To Face)

Align your body to the magnetic flow.

IF BREATH IS...	FACE THIS WAY	AVOID THIS WAY	BEST FOR
RIGHT (Sun)	East / North	West / South	Asking for money, Debating, War.
LEFT (Moon)	West / South	East / North	Proposals, Apologies, Healing.

4. The Phonetic Decoder (Name Compatibility)

Match the Name to the Breath.

NAME STARTS WITH	ELEMENT	BEST BREATH TO ENGAGE
K, G, T, D, R	Solar (Hard)	RIGHT (Sun)

S, Ch, J, L, M, N	**Lunar (Soft)**	**LEFT (Moon)**
Vowels (A, E, I...)	**Ether (Soft)**	**LEFT (Moon)**

FINAL WORD

"The Map is Complete. But the Journey is Not Over."

You have reached the end of The Instant Oracle.

You now possess a power that was once the secret of kings.

You can predict the outcome of a battle before the first shot is fired.

You can find lost objects in the dark.

You can look at a stranger and know their elemental nature.

You are no longer flying blind. You have radar.

But...

Prediction is passive.

Knowing the future is powerful, but changing the future is god-like.

- You know the deal will fail (Shunya). But can you force it to succeed?
- You know the person is angry (Fire). But can you transmute their anger into love?
- You know the disease is present. But can you heal it with a look?

There is one final level of Swara Yoga.

It is the level of Siddhi (Supernatural Power).

It is where the Yogi stops being a Reader and becomes a Writer.

He stops reading the script of destiny and starts editing it in real-time.

He learns to Transmit.

He learns to throw his Prana into another person's body to heal them, or to influence their thoughts.

He learns the ultimate secret of Tantric Alchemy—using the breath to merge two souls into one.

In Book 3: The Social Alchemist, we leave the realm of Observa-

tion.
We enter the realm of Influence.
We will learn:

- Remote Healing: Sending Prana across distance.
- Thought Transmission: Planting ideas on the breath.
- The Death of Ego: The ultimate union of Shiva and Shakti.

The Oracle has spoken.
Now, the Alchemist must act.
Turn the page. The transmutation begins.
— Kanav Sachdev
Om Namah Shivaya.

www.ingramcontent.com/pod-product-compliance
Lightning Source LLC
La Vergne TN
LVHW030911080826
845145LV00010B/2856

* 9 7 8 8 1 9 9 7 5 1 8 9 7 *